*R*aising
Godly Kids

52 GUIDELINES FOR
COUNTER–CULTURE
PARENTING

Raising Godly Kids

52 GUIDELINES FOR COUNTER−CULTURE PARENTING

HAROLD J. SALA

OMF LITERATURE INC.
Manila, Philippines

Cover design by Amor Aurelio Alvarez

Published (2002) in the Philippines by
OMF Literature Inc.
776 Boni Avenue
Mandaluyong City, Metro Manila
www.OMFLit.com

Reprinted — 2002 (twice), 2003 (thrice), 2004, 2005, 2006 (twice), 2007

ISBN 978-971-511-728-9

Printed in the Philippines

CONTENTS

PREFACE

The child you bring into the world is unique. He or she has no replica, not even his twin. Your baby is one of a kind. At conception, 500 million sperms competed with each other to fertilize the ovum. Twenty-three chromosomes from you and the same number from your mate combined to give your child unique features inherited from both sides of the family.

Apart from spiritual rebirth, nothing is more awesome than this marvelous phenomenon of reproducing ourselves in this little six- to eight-pound bundle of life. A baby is God's gift of life. But it is merely a loan to us. We don't own our children; we simply have eighteen years to pack their suitcases before they embark on life's journey.

Once we become parents, our lives will never be the same! Looking at that tiny bundle of joy in the hospital, no first-time parents have any concept—not even in their wildest imagination—of how their world is about to change forever. We soon learn that it's easy to be parents—at least for most of us—but difficult to be really good ones!

Parenting is one of the most awesome and demanding tasks of life with its ups and downs, challenges and surprises, tears and joys. With recent changes in our world and our culture (how do you tell your children that immorality and dishonesty are wrong when national leaders admit to both?), the responsibility of raising moral, God-fearing children in a world that flouts Christian values, often ignores civility and decency, and laughs at traditional values becomes more difficult—but certainly not impossible! God is still in the business of helping parents who are committed to Him. Just ask His help and follow the guidelines of Scripture.

I feel for couples who—for whatever reason—are unable to have children. I pity couples who willfully choose not to have children. They deprive themselves of the laughters, smiles, tears, bumps and certainly joys of a child growing to maturity.

The selections in this book are not definitive—not a manual on how to do it—but guidelines and insights that will help you be a better parent. These guidelines often underline the obvious, which, at times is obscured by the stress and the busyness of life today. As you read these practical selections you will be reminded that you are the value system your youngster will adopt. Values are caught than taught! I hope you will take time to ponder the insights at the end of each chapter and apply these to your parenting.

There are no second chances with parenting! If you fail, you can't go back and start over. You live with the consequences. You have no chance to practise at parenting. Yet your are embarking on what can be one of the most challenging and satisfying experiences of your life. I know, because my wife and I have raised three children who are now raising their own children very much as they were raised. And if I live long enough to see our grandchildren do the same thing, only then will I feel that I have really succeeded in this business of parenting.

Having been involved with families as a counselor, lecturer, family conference speaker and Bible teacher for more than four decades, I admit that with each passing year it becomes more challenging for godly parents to battle against an ungodly world, and raise kids so strong they won't need their parents when they are not there. You quickly learn as a parent that there will always be tension between Christian values and the world in which your child grows up. Knowing how to intervene (but not overreact) when necessary, in love and compassion, requires the skill of a diamond cutter and the balance of a tightrope walker. But with God's help you can do what needs to be done. You can raise godly children in an ungodly world!

Withdrawing from our world is not an option. Confronting the culture and raising your children to know and love the Lord is not only your responsibility before God, but can also be your greatest joy in life, your most important ministry and your most lasting and significant accomplishment.

Children are God's way of saying, "Life must go on, and I want your children to walk with Me and to learn that I am sufficient for them today, just as I was sufficient for you a generation ago!"

I recommend that as you read each selection, look up the resource passages, meditate on what you have read and strive to apply the guidelines to your child.

Be encouraged, friend! You can make a difference in the life of your child!

Harold J. Sala

ACKNOWLEDGMENTS

Apart from the input and assistance of many people, books as this would not be possible. My special thanks to Maynard Eyestone who originally proofed the selections which were written for *Guidelines—A Five-Minute Commentary*. As we rewrote and adapted these for this book, Luisa Ampil provided generous assistance in editing and printing.

I would also like to extend my gratitude to Barbour Publishing for the use of three selections included in this book—"Growing a Kid So Strong He Won't Need You When You Aren't There," "Raising Positive Kids in a Negative World" and "Growing Kids God's Way"—which are from my devotional book *Tomorrow Starts Today*.

My thanks also goes to Ramon Rocha and Yna Reyes, CEO, and Editorial Manager, respectively, of OMF Literature Inc. for making this book possible.

OUR GREATEST MISSION FIELD

*Like arrows in the hands of a warrior
are sons born in one's youth.
Psalm 127:4*

T he world's greatest mission field is not the vast continent of Africa, nor the highlands of Papua New Guinea nor the jungles of South America—as needy as those places are. Are you ready for this? The greatest mission field today is the hearts of our children. Today, forces more sinister than jungle vipers, and more devastating than medicine-resistant malaria are making bids for our children.

Our children are both our greatest challenge and our greatest mission field. But here is the question: How do we respond to the evil forces that challenge them? Turn off the TV set and strive to include them in your over-loaded schedule? Give them the gift of yourself? Yes, but there's more.

For a long while we parents have depended on others to do what we alone can do. We have expected the school, the church and other social institutions to convey values and provide an educational framework. We have expected our offspring to absorb whatever is necessary to succeed in life, and we have paid for it—tuition for education, music lessons, karate and sports. We have given them computers, TVs, eighteen-speed bicycles, basketballs and the latest digital audio equipment. But we have often neglected the personal element of parental love and the deeper lessons of what life is all about, including the spiritual.

I've often said that values in life are caught—not taught. I still believe that, but I also believe that the gift of parental love—the strong kind that includes caring enough to be there and to provide discipline and guidance until the children are old enough to make good decisions—is the only thing that will get kids through the jungle out there.

> *One of the greatest gifts parents can give their child is to love each other.*

When children know that they are loved and accepted regardless of what happens, this gives them stability that makes it much easier for them to stand on their own. As parents our goal should be to help our kids grow so strong that they won't need us. That can only be done through patient guidance, discipline and love.

What is the gift of love? Simply put, it is the gift of yourself. What kids today are worried about is not the earth being blown away by nuclear fission or not having enough to eat, but whether their Daddy and Mommy will stay together. The fear of separation has now become one of the greatest fears of children. <u>One of the greatest gifts parents can give their child is to love each other.</u>

A note left on the teacher's desk read, "Teacher, I need a hug. At the end of the day, would you please give me a hug? I know you'd rather be hugging your own children but I'm hurting. Love, Becky." Becky was an eleven-year-old girl, overweight and desperate for love. Her mother had divorced her husband because she wanted her independence. Becky's elderly grandmother was raising her the best that she could. But no one can really take the place of a mother or a father.

INSIGHT

Our first and greatest mission field is our children, and if we fail here, we register our greatest defeat.

Psychiatrist Dr. Ross Campbell, author of the book *How to Really Love Your Children* which has more than half a million copies in print, says that he has never treated an adolescent involved in sexual misconduct who felt loved by his parents. <u>Especially important is the love of a father.</u> Interestingly enough, the first mention of the word *love* in the Bible is that of a father's love for his son. The father was Abraham and the son was Isaac.

Could Becky be your child, desperately in need of love?

THINK ON THIS

1   Realize that your children are not a hindrance to your ministry. To the contrary, they are your ministry. Prioritize your time and energies appropriately.

2   Don't feel that time with your family—your children in particular— is wasted time that keeps you away from your business, your friends or ministry. Time spent with your children is time building lives—raising godly kids in an ungodly world.

RESOURCE READING

Psalm 127

LOVE STARTS
AT HOME

*Take your son, your only son, Isaac, whom
you love, and go. . . Sacrifice him there,
as a burnt offering.*
Genesis 22:2

"What the world needs now is love, sweet love" goes the old song. It's still true, but it is not only the world—it's also our families, and our children in particular. A study of the blueprint for family living found in the Bible concludes that God intended the family to be a foretaste of heaven on earth, not a bit of hell as it often is. His plan is for the family—your family—to be a model of the kingdom of God on earth. What God expects of us in relationship to Himself, He expects in our relationships in the family. God, who is love, puts priority on love in our relationships.

Remember that Jesus grew up in a normal family. Based on Matthew 13, after Jesus, Mary and Joseph reared seven more children. As the eldest in a brood of eight, Jesus likewise experienced all the frustrations of family living that puts us under stress today.

Most family arguments start over trivial things, like who didn't clean up the mess in the kitchen or who squeezed the toothpaste in the middle. Why is it that we often feel family members don't count when it comes to demonstrating and showing love—Christian love and commitment? Why do we feel that we can speak to each other at home in a tone that would cause our neighbors to punch our noses?

Real love embraces sacrifice.

There is no question that Jesus taught love as the test that a life has been touched with God's presence. In the Upper Room, immediately before His ascension to heaven, Jesus said, "Love each other as I have loved you" (John 15:12). In the same message He said, "By this all men will know that you are my disciples, if you love one another" (13:35).

Here's the definition of love that I like best: Love is an unconditional commitment to an imperfect individual to meet his or her needs even if it requires personal sacrifice. Real love— the kind that holds our families together—is not getting but giving; it embraces sacrifice, not simply indulging the one we love. This is not to suggest for a moment that in the beautiful relationship of marriage, love should not be expressed in the warmth and intimacy of sex—it's right and normal, but love goes much more beyond sex.

Love in the family is kept alive through little acts of kindness and thoughtfulness. The little kitchen motto, "Divine Service Performed Here Daily," has the right idea. Love is a commitment and a sacrament. It is the remedy to the sickness that has diseased our families and our lives. It is what your children need more than toys, computers, music lessons, clothes and anything else you can think of. And love starts at home—your home.

THINK ON THIS

One of the great characteristics of real love is discipline—not saying something but keeping quiet when necessary. Think of how you show love. Is the control of the tongue a measure of your love just as much as wiping a child's feverish brow, or cooking, cleaning and doing the laundry?

RESOURCE READING

Genesis 22

LATE STARTERS

After three days they found him in the temple courts, sitting among the teachers, listening to them and asking them questions. Everyone who heard him was amazed at his understanding and his answers.
Luke 2:46-47

Do you have a child who seems to have an attention deficit disorder? It's hard for him to sit still and doesn't pay attention to what the teacher is saying. He lives in his own private world, and doesn't seem to be interested in being with people. Before you see a doctor, give serious thought to the accomplishments of the following individuals who were considered slow learners or even retarded before their genius blossomed.

Late starter 1: Thomas Alva Edison eventually called "The Wizard of Menlo Park." When he was in grade school, his teacher wrote his mother that he should be transferred to remedial school because he was "inattentive, indolent" and his brain was "seriously addled." That incident ended his three months of formal education. The fact that Edison later became slightly deaf (perhaps the result of sharp blows to his head by a train conductor when Edison accidentally started a fire aboard a train) didn't help him to develop an out-going, pleasant personality either. But Edison was smart, real smart. He eventually became the most prolific inventor of all times.

Late starter 2: Hans Christian Andersen
Born in 1805, this young Dane wasn't worth "the powder to blow him to Helsinki," as one of his contemporaries put it. Yet he was a dreamer. After mediocre achievements in school, he became a ham actor. Then, at the age of thirty, he wrote *Eventyr*, a story for children, and his literary career began. Today everyone knows the fairy tales of Hans Christian Andersen.

Unless you are willing to let a youngster be an original, you will never know what he might blossom into.

Late starter 3: Louis Pasteur
He was a French lad often described as lazy and undirected. And that he was, preferring to wander in the fields and go fishing than do serious academic study. But in his twenties, he developed a fascination for science. Eventually Louis Pasteur's discovery, called pasteurization, saved the lives of thousands of children who otherwise would have died from drinking contaminated milk.

Late starter 4: Otto von Bismarck

If you've never heard of him, obviously you aren't German, because this great man took his place in history as "the Iron Chancellor" and gave his country hope in dark days. As a youth, however, Bismarck had little promise of success. He was described as a boy "who seemed destined for oblivion. His student life was spent in fighting, wenching and drinking." He is said to have given up alcohol in his twenties because it could no longer make him drunk. Until age thirty, his life seemed to be wasted. Then his values changed. He went into government, and history tells the rest of the story.

> **INSIGHT**
>
> *Every child's maturation rate differs. Some children considered slow are merely late starters.*

The bottom line is that lots of children are "slow starters." But that doesn't mean they are dull or hyperactive. They may just be unchallenged. Many are bored, not simply inattentive. Sometimes they are two jumps ahead of their teacher, who complains because the youngster "isn't paying attention."

No two children develop at the same rate. What his big brother or his big sister did at the same age shouldn't be expected of him. As a parent, you should strive to find out where your kids' interests and talents are and help develop them. Kids learn from their failures, and unless you are willing to let a youngster be an original, one who isn't like the rest of the kids in his class, you will never know what he might blossom into.

Not all the great leaders in history were child prodigies. But most had parents—at least a mother—who believed there was something great inside their child and were determined to help their child discover what it was.

Never underestimate the awesome, often un-discovered potential of a child. A Thomas Edison, an Albert Einstein, or a Jose Rizal may be waiting to be unleashed.

THINK ON THIS

1   Every child has gifts and abilities.
    Find out where your child excels and
    encourage him or her without
    ignoring the fundamentals of
    education.
2   Avoid the danger of comparing your
    late starters with other children.
3   If you feel that your late starter has a
    learning disability, get professional help.

RESOURCE READING

1 Samuel 1

DEVELOPING YOUR CHILD'S POTENTIAL

Then [Moses'] sister asked Pharaoh's daughter,
"Shall I go and get one of the Hebrew women to
nurse the baby for you?" "Yes, go," she answered.
And the girl went and got the baby's mother.
Pharaoh's daughter said to her, "Take this baby
and nurse him for me, and I will pay you."
Exodus 2:7-9

Are some people born with genius ability? Or are geniuses the product of their environment? Is there something in the childhood of some children that triggers intense brain development? After Einstein died, scientists examined his brain to see how it was different from other people's, but their prodding didn't really prove anything.

Before you consign your child to the category of "just average," let me quote Glenn Doman, the director of the Institute for the Achievement of Human Potential. He has demonstrated amazing results working with babies and preschool-age children. (Try teaching your two-year-old to read, as Dr. Doman and his colleagues have done!). He says, "Every child born has, at the moment of birth, a greater potential intelligence than Leonardo da Vinci ever used."[1]

In the context of what we know about the expanding human potential, this means that no one can know what tremendous, unheard-of or even unthought-of potential lies in that little bundle you have brought into the world.

Are you interested in bringing out the best in your child? The following guidelines are for you.

1 The gift of yourself is the greatest gift you can ever give your child.

While talking to an educator, I asked, "What is the most important thing a parent can do to bring out the best in a child?" Did this gifted professor talk about the importance of computers or books or expensive tutoring? No. The reply was simply,

> *The greatest thing that parents can give a child is themselves.*

"The greatest thing that parents can give a child is themselves." She labeled many parents as selfish, too concerned with their own plans and interests to be able to give of themselves to their children.

Children who excel usually have parents who read to them, spend time with them, are involved in school functions, believe in them, and include them in their lives. The child isn't the hub of parents' existence and their world doesn't rotate on the axis of their child's schedule, but the child knows that his parents care.

2 Bring out the best in your child by fostering your child's sense of curiosity.

Don't give him a pat answer when you can stir up his curiosity to discover the answer for himself. A recent Nobel Prize winner said that his research in the field of science was the result of his mother's encouragement to find out what makes things tick.

If you don't know the answer yourself, help your youngster connect with those who do. As a boy, my son Steve was fascinated with electronics, a field I knew very little about. But I introduced Steve to Byrd Brunemeier, who was a brilliant electrical engineer. I bought the transistors and components and Byrd helped him learn to put them together. Today Steve is a biomedical engineer!

> **INSIGHT**
>
> *While you as a parent cannot do a great deal to increase your child's IQ, you can make a great difference in satisfying his CQ (curiosity quotient).*

3 Help your child to develop faith in God and a moral foundation that can guide his life.

Apart from this we can produce gifted children who are morally bankrupt. Bringing out the potential in your child includes teaching him how to live, not just how to make a living. This includes the moral, the physical and the spiritual. Integrity, honesty, trustworthiness and faithfulness are all part of what counts in life. Never, never forget that.

THINK ON THIS

1   Thomas Edison said that his achievements were not the result of his great intelligence but of his tenacity and persistence. How do you handle the "Where?" and "How?" questions of your smaller children?

2   Answering a child's question is good. But helping a child discover the answer for himself is much better.

3   What resources do you have in your home to help develop your child's potential? A word of warning: Unscrupulous individuals taking advantage of your desire to give the best to your child may strive to sell you "a bill of goods" which is practically worthless

when it comes to real educational benefit. Before you buy, check with parents who have used those resources.

4   If you don't know how to use the Internet for research, find out. Check out web sites such as www.askjeeves.com.

Resource Reading

John 1:41-51

THE EFFECTIVENESS OF "PROGRAM MOM"

As a mother comforts her child,
so will I comfort you; and you will be
comforted over Jerusalem.
Isaiah 66:13

I n the last decade," writes Delbert Elliott in an article entitled "How Could This Happen?" "we have achieved a major breakthrough in our understanding of the causes and prevention of youth violence... Research has succeeded in demonstrating the effectiveness of selected programs in preventing or deterring crime and violence."[2]

While my comments are not meant to detract from the merits of these programs, I am glad to tell you that there is an old program which is still unrivaled in its effectiveness. It is called "Program Mom," and applied in the right places and at the proper times, no program in the entire world can equal its power!

When Program Mom is working, there is a proper tension between love and compassion on the one hand, and motivation and persuasion on the other hand. I had the most wonderful mother in the world, yet there were times when she could be downright cruel, insisting that I practice my music lessons and that I take a bath (at least on Saturday nights). She insisted that I eat at least a spoonful of everything that was served, actually trying to convince me and my equally disbelieving brother that spinach was good for us and that turnips and beets are nutritious (I remain un-convinced to this day).

Seldom did Mom ever cry, but one time she did. My brother and I will never forget it. That was when my dad brought my mother a vase from Marshall Fields in Chicago. A baseball thrown poorly by one of us went astray and hit the vase, sending that lovely, frilly blue vase to the floor in more pieces than Humpty Dumpty's men could ever put together again.

Dad ranted and raved and gave us lectures which

When Program Mom is working, there is a proper tension between love and compassion on the one hand, and motivation and persuasion on the other hand.

we promptly forgot, but Mom prayed for us, loved us and showed us that a mother can be involved in business, run the family, listen to us and still manage to keep a sense of humor.

I have never seen her so angry as the time a man lied to her, telling her that the woman he was with was his wife, when, in fact, he was checking into the motel my parents owned with someone else. Calling him on the phone, she said, "I'll give you five minutes to get out of here, and if you are not gone by then, I am calling your wife to tell her where you are." Believe me, that man and that woman never dressed so fast in their lives.

Good stuff, that program my mom had. Mothers who mother their children are the greatest program God ever invented. When Program Mom gets into full operation, demons tremble, and kids learn very quickly that the fury of a tornado is not her equal. Yes, government programs might help, but give us more Program Moms!

> ## INSIGHT
>
> *All mothers are human, yet with all their failures, they are one of God's greatest gifts to us. If you are a mother, remember that you are coming through even when you have bad days.*

Think on This

1   Don't expect to walk on water. Your mother didn't and neither will you. Each day strive to be the mother who makes a difference in the life of your youngster.

2   You must realize that when your schedule gets loaded and you find yourself uptight and stressed out, you transfer your tension to your child. His behavior will merely reflect your attitude. Back off. Take a deep breath and get a new grip on yourself and God.

Resource Reading

Proverbs 31

ACCEPTING RESPONSIBILITY FOR YOUR CHILDREN

For what will it profit a man
if he gains the whole world,
and loses his own soul?
Mark 8:36 NKJV

ach June we set aside one Sunday to honor dads. We call it Father's Day. Naturally dads think this is a great idea. But there is a tragic aspect to it too, because the failure of fathers today is an enormous social blight.

A great many fathers have only themselves to blame. They weren't there for their kids because they were climbing the corporate ladder, striving to prove their self-worth and making money to be able to live "the good life." The son of a prominent executive described his dad "a Phi Beta Kappa, a Rhodes scholar and a company president who flunked marriage, fatherhood, friendship and fun."

Jesus said, "What will it profit a man if he gains the whole world, and loses his own soul?" (Mark 8:36, *NKJV*). He might add, "What will it profit a man if he gains the company presidency and loses his family in the process?"

Is success—the kind that leads to membership in the club, the car and status—really worth the cost?

The *Wall Street Journal*, together with the Gallup Organization, once did a survey of the heads of 780 major corporations, focusing on their work habits and attitudes and how men in the US cope with the pressures in relation to their marriages and their children. The survey was

Home and family come only second for the typical corporate executive.

based on interviews with CEOs among the 1,300 largest corporations. It also included 100 of the Fortune 500 companies, 276 heads of medium-size companies and 198 independent owners of small businesses.

And how are men coping with success? The survey delivers an unmistakable verdict: Home and family come only second for the typical corporate executive.

Among the specific findings: Chief executives typically work sixty to seventy hours a week, travel six to ten days a month and give up many of their weekends for business meetings. Having made it to the top, two out of every three executives said they were convinced the pressures were greater and the cost to their family more severe than when they were middle managers. One company president said, "I gave my family everything in the world but myself."

Your children are pleading, "Dear Dad, please give us yourself, your time and your undivided attention. Please show us the way by being there, by listening when we need to talk, by giving us guidance when we stray, by being God's man so we can understand who we are and who God is."

> INSIGHT
>
> *A man's greatest achievement is not what he does in business but what he does with his marriage and family.*

"Daddy, how much do you make an hour?" asked one little boy. And his father told him. Five minutes later, the boy appeared with his piggy bank and said, "Daddy, here's all my money—just half of what you make in an hour. Now can I have you for just thirty minutes?"

The whole experience of being a father goes by so quickly that you look back and ask, "Where was I when my child was growing up?" There are no second chances, no retakes—only memories. The best intentions will never suffice for missed opportunities. If God has made you a dad, rise to the challenge. You'll never regret it.

Think on This

1   If you had told your son you'd be watching their school program and your boss asked you to have lunch with an important client at the same time, what would you do? Would you feel torn?

2   A wife complained that her husband was "never there" for the children as they grew up. He retorted, "No, because you were never satisfied with my salary so I had to work longer hours to make you happy." What is wrong in this situation?

3   Have you and your spouse ever sat down and evaluated your priorities? You might start with your finances. We spend money on what we consider important.

Resource Reading

Proverbs 3

DAD, PLEASE LOVE US

*If anyone does not provide for his own,
and especially for those of
his household, he has denied the faith
and is worse than an unbeliever.*
1 Timothy 5:8, NKJV

A father may provide leadership for his family without love, but he cannot love them without leadership. Love is not a wishy-washy emotion associated with weak-kneed men. It is costly but it provides the family with the strength it needs to withstand the storm.

"Dad, please love us!" We previously pointed out that the first mention of the word "love" in the Bible is that of a father's relationship to his son—Abraham's love for his son Isaac.

When Jesus was on earth in the flesh, He surrounded Himself with twelve men—men who were men—and told them to love one another as He Himself loved them. It was not a sickly, sentimental love and certainly not sexual love, but a deep commitment to one another which reflected care and concern.

Paul instructed men to "love their wives as their own bodies" (Ephesians 5:28). Long ago Jeremy Taylor wrote, "He that loves not his wife and children feeds a lioness at home and broods a nest of sorrow."

Psychologist Dr. Irene Kassorla, writing for *Family Circle* magazine, says, "I urge parents to kiss and embrace their sons and forget our ... nonsense concerning the male macho image! Affection acts as an emotional growth stimulant. Everyone needs it, regardless of age or sex!"

If you love someone, you care for that person—which is why Paul wrote that husbands should love their wives as their own bodies. Writing to Timothy, Paul penned some pretty strong words when he wrote this: "If anyone does not provide for his own,

> *"He that loves not his wife and children feeds a lioness at home and broods a nest of sorrow."*

and especially for those of his household, he has denied the faith and is worse than an unbeliever" (1 Timothy 5:8, *NKJV*).

In his book *If I Were Starting My Family Again*, author John Drescher asked himself what he would do if, as the book title suggests, he were starting all over again. He answers that question:

"I would love the mother of my children more. That is, I would be more free to let my children see that I love her. To let my child know that I love his mother, I would seek to be faithful in doing little loving things for her. True love is visible. I would show special kindness such as opening the car door, placing a chair at the table, and giving her little gifts on special occasions and writing her love letters when I am gone from home.... When a child knows parents love each other there is a security, stability and sacredness about life which is gained in no

other way. A child who knows that his parents love each other and hears them expressing words of love for each other needs little explanation about God's character of love or the beauty of sex."[3]

One closing thought: It is well and good to talk about love's commitment, care and concern, but love does not come in capsules or in doses. It is born in your heart as God touches your life. Do you want to love your wife and your children more? Then love God more and the latter will follow. "God," wrote Paul, "has poured out His love into our hearts by the Holy Spirit, whom He has given us" (Romans 5:5).

"Yes, Dad, please love us!" Signed, "Your family."

THINK ON THIS

1 Do you hug and kiss your children? If not, why?
2 Are you and your spouse together in affirming the importance of your love for each other? If not, is this not a problem that needs to be addressed?

RESOURCE READING

2 Timothy 2:1-7

DAD, PLEASE
LISTEN TO US

*He who answers before listening—that is
his folly and his shame.*
Proverbs 18:13

My dad won't listen to me!" says a
frustrated teenager. I do not know how
many times I have heard those words, at
times coming from teenagers whose fathers I
know personally. I know that the father really does
love his child. He would die for her. So why doesn't
he listen?

Perhaps he does listen but there is a conflict of
signals. The daughter interprets his answer, "No,
you cannot do this," as repressive. Or perhaps the
father does not really listen. Perhaps he is too
tired at the end of the day; perhaps he no longer
has the emotional energy to be an effective
communicator. Or perhaps he just doesn't care
about what she is saying.

One of the most important things you can do as
a father is to turn off the TV set, put down the

newspaper and give your undivided attention to your children. Listen without being judgmental or reproving. If you want to become the father God wants you to be, learn to listen to your children. If you do, they will listen to you when they become teenagers and young adults.

I am thinking of one dad who was reading his paper as his little boy, about five years old, was trying to show his father the scratch on his finger. Finally, after repeated attempts to get his father's attention, the dad stopped reading and half-yelled, "Well, I cannot do anything about it, can I?"

One of the most important things you can do as a father is to give your undivided attention to your children.

"Yes, Daddy," the little guy said, "you could have said, 'Oh!'"

Do you want to know how to be a better communicator, Dad? Then take note of the following guidelines:

1 Realize you must recognize the absolute necessity of listening to your family.
It means flopping down on the bed with your teen-ager and asking, "How did your day go?" It means being willing to spend time and energy when you would rather be sleeping or reading. It means that listening is a vital part of being a Christian dad.

2 Learn to listen without intimidating your child. There are times when judgmental attitudes or "iron-fisted pronouncements" put an abrupt end to the communication. That does not mean that there is not a time and a way in which you can give correction or guidance, but often it is not when you should be trying to listen.

> **INSIGHT**
>
> *Listening is a teaching experience. You convey your belief that the person you are listening to—whether it is a four-year-old or a business associate —is a person of value and worth. Listening says, "I care about you enough to give you my complete, undivided attention."*

3 Show a sincere interest in what your family wants to talk about. If you live in your own little world, you are apt to find yourself pretty lonely in a few years. I have come to the conclusion that at every stage of life the immediate challenge is the greatest. To a four-year-old, it may be the broken toy he holds in his hand; to a forty-year-old, it may be a company merger. But the child's problem is as great to him as the business problem is to his dad.

In the final analysis, listening requires a certain posture of the heart, a certain humility of the spirit, a certain interest in someone other than yourself. Give your children your undivided attention, and listen. It fulfills a deep and basic need. Dad, your family is crying, "Lead us, love us and listen to us." It is a plea that you cannot afford to ignore.

THINK ON THIS

1   If you are brave, sit down with your older children and discuss, "On a scale of 1 to 10, how would you rate me as a listener?"

2   Dad, if your child had a problem, would he:
    (a) Tell your wife?
    (b) Tell you?
    (c) Tell a friend?
    If he would not tell you, why not?

3   The stage has to be set for the "listening" experience, which means

focusing on the needs of the child and ignoring the distractions of the household. Take note of those nonverbal signals that say, "I would like to tell you something." It's amazing what you may discover.

RESOURCE READING

2 Timothy 4:10-17

MISTAKES PARENTS CAN'T AFFORD TO MAKE

*The wolf also shall dwell with the lamb, and
the leopard shall lie down with the kid; and
the calf and the young lion and the fatling
together; and a little child shall lead them.*
Isaiah 11:6, KJV

No parent lives long enough to make all the mistakes in the book, but having been through the process three times over, I've learned there are some mistakes you can't afford to make. The following are statements which should never—no exceptions—come from the lips of a parent.

1 "Do what I say, not what I do!"

Forget it. Your example cancels out everything you say. Your kids need role models, not sermons. If you don't measure up, forget the rhetoric and concentrate on your example.

2 "Here's a gift—I can't be there with you."

Gifts are poor substitutes for your presence. Being at the ball game or at the school function, even though it is a sacrifice of time and energy, means more than the reward you may give to your son or daughter.

3 "If you do this again, you're going to get it."

A major blunder! Consistency is one of the most necessary components of parenting. When you do not deal with a situation and discipline a child right away—no matter how tired you are—you are sending conflicting signals. This produces uncertainty.

Teaching a child to be responsible is planting the seeds of future success.

Consistent and definite boundaries give stability and security to a child.

4 "Because I love you, I'm doing this for you."

Love isn't the issue. Responsibility is. Failure to teach your children to assume responsibility for their lives ill prepares them for the future. Later on, college roommates, bosses or spouses won't do it for them. Teaching a child to be responsible is planting the seeds of future success.

5 "How could you be so dumb?"

Telling a child what he did wrong only certifies the obvious. It's better to talk about how to handle a troublesome situation in the future. Saying, "Let's talk about how you are going to handle this the next time" lets you deal with character building.

6 "If your older brother can get high grades, why can't you?"
Comparing children creates anger and defensiveness. Every child is different. Each has aptitudes and abilities which may be lacking in other children—even children of the same parents. Strive to recognize what each child does well and build on that. That's what the Scripture is driving at when it says, "Train a child in the way he should go" (Proverbs 22:6).

> **INSIGHT**
> *Sarcasm and negative comments are always wrong. They produce anger, not correction; resentment, not instruction. Take a deep breath and pause for a moment before you say what you want to say—this can prevent you from coming up with one of these ten negative statements.*

7 "If you don't stop that, I'll tell your father when he gets home."
Discipline should be administered immediately, not later when the other parent is around.

8 "If you are a good child, I'll give you some extra money!"

Rewards for doing the right thing teach the wrong thing. Doing right is a responsibility—yes, even a duty. It isn't always rewarded in life by pay increases or bonuses. Teaching children to do right because it is right is responsible parenting.

9 "God's going to get you when you are bad!"

Parents who use God as the "bogeyman" are teaching the wrong thing about God. Understanding that there is forgiveness with God as well as with each other is an important spiritual truth.

10 "When you get old enough to choose for yourself, you can go to church."

Wrong again! A child learns half of everything he knows by age three, three-fourths by age seven. The spiritual training of a child begins at birth.

Nobody's perfect, but these are some mistakes you can't afford to make.

THINK ON THIS

Do you find yourself saying stupid things—things which you really don't mean but say because you are under stress, in a hurry or plain annoyed? Disciplining yourself is the key to teaching a child how to discipline himself.

RESOURCE READING
Genesis 20

OUT OF THE MOUTHS OF BABES

*The things that come out of the
mouth come from the heart.*
Matthew 15:18

A husband came home to find his wife in tears. "What's the matter, honey?" he asked. "Let me tell you," she began "Today Junior cut his first tooth and took his first step."

"That sounds wonderful," said the baby's father. "Why the tears?"

"Well," continued the wife, "he also had his first fall and cut his lip, and when he did, he said his first bad word."

There is nothing funny about the implications of a situation a *Guidelines* listener described when he wrote: "I am experiencing a terrible, terrible temper. I can get very violent and I curse and yell very loud. What makes this behavior even worse is that I have a two-year-old who now says curse words, and a month-old baby who will learn them if I can't stop this behavior."

Out of the mouths of babes may come words which will shock hearers, words which innocent children neither understand

The real failure that confronts our children today is our failure as parents to provide an example for our children to follow.

nor mean. We parents, by our examples, are the teachers of our children. It is both unfair of us to discipline a child for using words he learned from us.

In my file is an article by an unknown author which says it so clearly:

"If a child lives with criticism,
   he learns to condemn.
If a child lives with hostility,
   he learns to fight.
If a child lives with ridicule,
   he learns to be shy.
If a child lives with shame,
   he learns to feel guilty.
If a child lives with tolerance,
   he learns to be patient.
If a child lives with encouragement,
   he learns confidence.
If a child lives with praise,
   he learns to appreciate.

If a child lives with fairness,
    he learns justice.
If a child lives with security,
    he learns to have faith.
If a child lives with approval,
    he learns to like himself.
If a child lives with acceptance and
friendship,
                he learns to find
                love in the world."

INSIGHT

It is unfair to expect our children to adopt a standard which we ourselves fail to meet. If you fail in a certain area, begin by asking for God's forgiveness and help, then look at the stress in your life. Learn to pour out your frustration in prayer. Join a support group. Talk.

We may condemn schools for failing to provide a wholesome environment for learning. We may condemn the media for the steady diet of anti-family values. But the real failure that confronts children today is the failure of parents to provide an example for children to follow. Yes, I understand the stress and frustration of a single parent, pressed by inadequate finances, wearied by the constant push of the schedule and the loneliness of doing it alone. But the real problem confronting our children today is us. When we parents have our act together, our kids are more secure. When we ourselves learn discipline, our children require less discipline. When we learn how to accept the circumstances of our lives, our children learn to cope with the frustrations that surround them.

When Jesus talked about the issues of life, He always spoke of the heart. He stressed the fact that what we say and do are expressions of what we have in our hearts. In doing verbal combat with His detractors who wanted to observe the legalism of washing their hands when their hearts were impure, Jesus said,

> "The things that come out of the mouth come from the heart.... For out of the heart come evil thoughts, murder, adultery, sexual immorality, theft, false testimony, slander. These are what make a man unclean; but eating with unwashed hands does not make him unclean." (Matthew 15:18-20)

If you, as a parent, are struggling with your own personal life, get help. Remember, it is your heart, not your mouth, which is the real issue.

THINK ON THIS

It is amazing how children read us adults—sensing our anger, our frustration, our compassion and our concern—and then emulate our attitudes and emotions. Should you fail, apologize—right away—for your failure, thereby teaching an important lesson in humility. Then strive to say and do the right things.

RESOURCE READING

Matthew 15

START 'EM YOUNG

And Jesus grew in wisdom and stature,
and in favor with God and men.
Luke 2:52

T he time to start a child on a musical career should not be too far beyond the bootie and bottle age—so says the increasingly popular Suzuki method of teaching music. This method, conceptualized by Dr. Shinichi Suzuki of Japan, is based on the idea that the earlier the child is exposed to music, the better a musician he will be. Just as a child imitates gestures, he can also imitate music. While Dr. Suzuki likes to start his students between the ages of two and four, he begins exposing them to music even earlier.

If the value of early training is so vital in music, how much more is this true in regard to your child's character! Dr. Suzuki says it is extremely important that a child hear nothing but good music from a very early age so that he develops a sense of harmony and rhythm.

What do children hear in your home? I am not talking about just music, but everything. Is it good? What do they listen to on TV and radio? What kind of language do they hear? Your child will forget a great deal of what you tell him, but he will never forget the example you set in your life. At a very early age he knows what is important to you—whether it is your job, your appearance, your home or whatever. You cannot start too early to create an environment at home

> *When God is real to you, He will be real to your children.*

that teaches the importance not only of good music but of values, such as honesty, integrity and respect for authority.

Going a step further, what does the example set in your home teach your children about God and the Bible? You may say, "Oh, I take my children to church every Sunday." Do you? That's good! Many parents do not feel it is important enough for them to bother. But what goes on in your home the other six days of the week? More and more, homes are places only to change clothes, eat and sleep.

Problems among children and youth are on the increase. We need all the help we can get in raising our children. Learn to take a few minutes each day to pray together as a family and to read a few verses from the Bible. You may feel awkward or even a little embarrassed or old-fashioned at first, but as you take the first step, God will help you.

When God is real to you, He will be real to your children. Do not be tricked into thinking that you can wait until they are older to teach them.

The Apostle Paul wrote two letters to Timothy. This young man Timothy was fortunate—his mother and grandmother who were both godly taught him the Word of God. He also sat under Paul's teaching. Of Timothy, Paul said that from childhood he knew the Holy Scriptures (see 2 Timothy 3:15). Could this be said of your children?

INSIGHT

In all of life's experiences we never learn more quickly and more diversely than we do in the first three or four years of life—the time to begin planting Scripture, integrity, moral uprightness and a sense of right and wrong.

You go to a great deal of work to raise your children. You teach them good health habits. You spend a great deal of money giving them a good education. Do not shortchange them when it comes to spiritual things. God's Word, the Bible, provides the spiritual guidance your children need in life. It builds integrity and gives them the guidelines to live useful, purposeful lives.

Listen to your three-year-old recite or sing back the commercials he hears on TV. Why not start planting Scripture and songs of the faith in your child's heart? Don't wait. Start 'em young as Dr. Suzuki does with budding musicians. You'll be glad you did!

Think on This

1   If you have a child under five, ask him, "Who was Moses? Who was the beautiful queen of Persia who rescued God's people from certain destruction? How many apostles did Jesus have? What does John 3:16 tell us?" Will your child know the answers?

2   What biblical resources do you have to help provide instruction and teaching for your children? If you are too tired to have devotions with your children at bedtime, decide what is the best time for you and dedicate a few minutes to it everyday.

Resource Reading

Luke 2:41-52

SPYING ON YOUR KIDS

*Don't keep on scolding and nagging your children,
making them angry and resentful. Rather, bring them
up with the loving discipline the Lord Himself
approves, with suggestions and godly advice.*
Ephesians 6:4, TLB

I s it OK to spy on your kids?" asked the
concerned parent of a teenager who isn't
talking much, at least to his parents. How far do
you go to find out what is going on in the life of
your teenager? Spying may include going through
your teenager's dresser drawers, reading his diary,
going into the files of his computer and reading
his e-mail (or mail) or otherwise investigating
what he thinks you will never see. How far is too
far? Does a teenager have a right not to tell as his
right to privacy?

These are some of the issues that are being
tackled today by parents who are concerned about
drugs, alcohol, sexual encounters, and being shut
out of their teen's world.

Years ago most parents knew what was going
on in the lives of their kids, and if they didn't

know, it was because they chose not to know. Today, however, it is different. Many of today's teenagers were raised with little contact with their parents. They were dropped off at childcare centers, brought home to empty houses and baby-sat by Nintendo and MTV. It is no wonder that today they give one-word answers to the indifferent questions of parents, rolling their eyes and saying whatever is necessary to get their parents off their backs.

A generation ago when we used the term "spy," we conjured images of Agent 007. You spy on the enemy, not your allies. When parents feel it is necessary to spy on their kids, they have drawn a line and put their offspring on the other side as an adversary.

> *When parents are there for their kids, they can generally read them like a book.*

A teenager doesn't suddenly transform into a silent stranger—he becomes a teenager one day at a time. When parents are there for their kids, they can generally read them like a book. They know when something is wrong, when there's something that needs to be talked about.

You don't have to be concerned about spying when you as a parent nurture the relationship you have with your offspring. You can foster this by doing things together, by participating in hobbies you both enjoy and by knowing what kind of music and books your teen likes. You can invite

your teen's friends over so you can get to know **them.** By having meals together as a family and by going to church together, you can even make it easy for your teen to spend time with friends that are good and not with kids that bring out the worst in him.

Says Dr. Laura Schlessinger, a popular, no-nonsense dispenser of personal advice:

> "Parents are to respect their children's nest and 'stuff.' However, when a parent has reason to believe that there might be a problem— sex, drugs, criminality, for example—it is their obligation to use whatever means necessary to help and protect their child."[4]

INSIGHT

Spying damages the relationship of trust you have with your child. However, if your teenager has violated that relationship, you have the responsibility to know what he is doing and thinking. But moving into the arena of surveillance brings consequences you need to think through before you start snooping.

I agree. Spying is a desperate, last-ditch measure of finding out what is happening in the life of your teenager. However, much better is straight-talk communication. Sometimes confrontation and a lot of being there shows you care.

When that kind of parenting is practiced, spying isn't necessary.

THINK ON THIS

1   If you are more comfortable not knowing what is going on in the life of your teenager, you are probably shirking from your responsibility to provide guidance and support. If you honestly don't want to know, why?

2   If your teenager flashes rolls of money and you have no idea where it comes from, how would you handle the situation? If you confront the issue and get a "Don't ask me 'cause I won't tell you," would that be reason to start investigating?

3   Under what circumstances would you feel justified in checking e-mail, phone messages, or desk drawers?

RESOURCE READING

1 Chronicles 6:1, 6-8

YOUR CHILDREN'S FUTURE

*And I will pour out on the house of David and the
inhabitants of Jerusalem a spirit of grace and
supplication. They will look on me, the one they have
pierced, and they will mourn for him
as one mourns for an only child, and grieve bitterly
for him as one grieves for a firstborn son.*
Zechariah 12:10

My name is Igor. If you find me, please
bring me to the following address,"
began a note Aida Cerkez wrote and
placed in the backpack of her two-year-old son.
Along with the note were two diapers, some crackers,
juice, Aida's life insurance policy and snapshots of
Igor and his mother and father.

Igor lived in Sarajevo. His mother was so
uncertain that she would be living by the end of the
day that she placed the backpack on the little boy
every morning. She said, "I thought that if we all get
killed, he could survive on his own for twenty-four
hours until someone found him, because I taught him
how to open his crackers."

Igor's mother was doing her best to prepare her
child to survive because she might not make it
herself. As I read about Igor, I couldn't help

thinking of my own little grandson William, who at the time was just about Igor's age. Just thinking of William with his little glasses perched on his nose, his baseball cap on his head and a backpack with crackers and a note inside brought tears to my eyes. I have no idea whether Igor and his mother survived. I hope they did.

There are no guarantees in our world. At times it's a pretty tough place to live. Yes, the fighting in Sarajevo had stopped, but the plight of Aida still takes place every day somewhere in this world.

I admired that mother for doing what she did, no matter how hard it may have been emotionally. Thinking about Igor made me think of what parents do for the future of their children. They provide food,

Do you think much about the spiritual heritage you are giving your child?

clothing, education, and recreation. They see to the physical and emotional needs of their children, but many stop right there.

I'm thinking of a mother of several children whose grandmother picked the children up on Sunday mornings and took them to church with her. The mother slept in on Sundays and did nothing to help the children get ready. "I don't believe in forcing God on my children," she told me. "When they get old enough, they can decide for themselves."

"Do you force them to go to school when they want to play hooky? Do you insist they take baths and medication when they're sick?" I asked.

It is no wonder we are living in a spiritual jungle today. Scores of young men and women drift without meaning and purpose in life. Somewhere in the process of growing up they were abandoned by parents who, not having found God, gave them little, if any, spiritual direction.

Do you think much about the spiritual heritage you are giving your child? Or should I say "denying" your child?

INSIGHT

God has given you the opportunity to lay a foundation for your children—much like the root system of a tree which can either go deep into the ground or remain in shallow ground.

Seeing to it that your child has a vibrant faith in God is just as vital as anything you could include in a knapsack to keep him alive until someone finds him.

We assume that our children will learn values just by growing up in a good home. Yet we don't apply that assumption to their education, health, sports or culture. You have eighteen years to pack your child's knapsack before he really faces the world. Make sure you've provided what he needs to survive.

THINK ON THIS

Your value system shapes the value system your child will have in his life. How seriously do you take this truth? Take some time for reflection. It's never too late to do a mid-course readjustment.

RESOURCE READING

Proverbs 20

PUBLIC SCHOOL, CHRISTIAN SCHOOL, OR HOME SCHOOL?

The sayings of King Lemuel—an oracle
his mother taught him.
Proverbs 31:1

Should you pull your youngster out of the secular system and put him into a Christian school? Many parents do—some at great financial cost—because they are convinced that putting their children in a school where God is in and evolution is out, where the days open with prayer, and where teachers are compassionate and caring is worth the personal sacrifice; knowing that their youngster will receive a solid academic foundation. So they make do with fewer clothes, longer working hours and lesser spendings, believing that their sacrifice will someday be rewarded.

Another option that has recently taken off like a locomotive running downhill is home schooling.

For years I was not very excited about private Christian education or home schooling. I felt that we as Christians need to be salt and light out there in the world where we can make a difference with our witness.

But as our culture darkened, sinister forces began to make our schools unsafe, and educational competence declined, I began to see how important private Christian schools can be. Knowing that a child is in a Christian environment where teachers are there because of commitment to Christian ideals is important. Teachers in Christian schools are usually motivated by their desire to make a difference in the lives of their students.

Why object to home schooling? I was not sure all moms could handle it academically, an issue which is still of some concern. I thought that only a superwoman could be teacher, mother and disciplinarian all wrapped up in one. I was also concerned about the youngster's

A growing home school movement brings mothers together, provides social outlets for the kids and provides a youngster an education which far exceeds anything public education can offer.

social development. But a growing home school movement brings mothers together, provides social outlets for the kids and provides the youngster an education that far exceeds anything public education can offer.

Home schooling frees a child from social competition—the "I've-got-to-be-just-like-everybody-else" mentality. It allows him an opportunity to follow Sir Edmund Hillary's wild ride in the ice and snow of the South Pole, retrace the route of the Lewis and Clark expedition or invent the incandescent globe, as Thomas Edison did.

> **INSIGHT**
>
> *Your child is going to get an education regardless of what happens. It may be one of academic excellence or mediocrity. However, no matter how good or poor the school system he may be in, your input as a parent makes a tremendous difference.*

I'm convinced that it can be very beneficial to the student as well as the mother, provided she has the temperament, the education and the time to handle the challenge.

If you have options, explore them fully. Make a list of pros and cons for each one. Lay them before the Lord and say, "Father, this child is a gift from You, and I want to help equip him to know You, love You and serve You all his life. Now, Lord, what's the best thing for us all?"

THINK ON THIS

1   Answering your child's questions: "Why do birds sleep in trees? How does electricity work? Why is the ocean salty?" provides learning experiences. Take the time to help your child find out the answers.

2   When you are exhausted it is OK to say, "Save that question until tomorrow and we'll find out." If your youngster forgets, remind him. He will care and be interested.

RESOURCE READING

Acts 13

SIT STILL, KID

*The power of the LORD came upon Elijah
and, tucking his cloak into his belt, he
ran ahead of Ahab all the way to Jezreel.*
1 Kings 18:46

Ryan, four years old, wriggled and squirmed during storytime at preschool, so he got sent to the office. His mother got a phone call reporting his lack of attention. The teacher asked her, "Have you talked to your doctor about this problem?" In other words, consider medicating the little guy.

Whoa! Just a minute! Any four-year-old is going to be active. Move! Wriggle! Squirm! That's the way a child's body was made! A less-than-exciting teacher says, "Now, sit still!" There's no question how the child is going to behave.

As many as one in twenty grade school youngsters in America today are being medicated daily. A visit to the doctor who may lack pediatric mental health training results in the diagnosis of ADHD (Attention Deficit Hyperactive Disorder) and probably a prescription for Ritalin.

Recently, Stanford University researchers demonstrated that there may be a difference in brain chemistry in some children diagnosed with ADHD. Unquestionably some children could not function in society without medical help. For them drugs such as Ritalin are helpful, but for the vast number of parents who think that giving a child a pill makes him a good boy, the route of medication is altogether too easy a solution.

Have our children become victims of ourselves, our stress, our frustrations, our busyness, our consumer-oriented lifestyles? We're working. We're too tired. We're too consumed with our own interests. We're too busy to throw a ball with our son in the backyard, or sew or bake or even shop together. So why not fix the problem with a pill?

Look at the whole picture before you head to the pharmacy and expect the medication to fix the problem.

The answer to so many of these problems is not biochemistry, valid as it is. It is changing our thinking and our lifestyle. But we can't turn back the clock of our culture. Neither are there easy solutions to the problems that confront parents today.

Pediatrician Dr. Kathi J. Kemper, who practices holistic medicine, tries to put the situation in perspective. She says,

> "In the old days, kids...learned from their parents around the home, farm or other business. There was a fair amount of movement, physical activity and parental involvement, without the modern cultural phenomenon of instant gratification. Nowadays, kids are bombarded with fastfood, frenetic television and video games. Modern schools increasingly demand that young children sit quietly in crowded classrooms with few breaks for vigorous physical activity. And busy families just don't have as much time to give children one-on-one attention."[5]

> ### INSIGHT
>
> *When medication is really needed, it is wonderful—a gift from God. But to medicate a child's inattention when he is bored, keyed-up because of inactivity, or fidgety when he is tired is wrong. The problem may well be your lifestyle as a parent.*

You as a parent must ultimately remember that you are Dr. Mom and Dr. Dad, and that you

know your child far better than an overworked
physician. Doctors can only take as much time to
evaluate your child as their schedule will allow them,
but they still won't have the whole picture. Talk.
Get more opinions. Explore alternatives to your
working outside the home. Take time to evaluate
how much time your child spends outdoors
compared to being in front of a TV or a computer
game. Look at the whole picture before you head
to the pharmacy and expect the medication to fix
the problem.

Ryan's mother (who is my daughter) didn't go to
the doctor. We attribute Ryan's wriggling to his
DNA. It seems his mother and his grandfather
(that's me) used to wriggle and squirm as well
when things got boring. Remember, when a child's
body says, "Wriggle," and you say, "Sit still," you've
got tough competition.

THINK ON THIS

1   There is safety in a multitude of
    counselors. Ask your mother how you
    were as a child.
2   Remember that every child's tempera-
    ment and personality is different.
    There are some children who sit

remarkably still. If God made your child with a tighter spring, that doesn't make him defective—just different.

Resource Reading

1 Samuel 2

THE DIAGNOSIS MAY BE WRONG

Who is this that darkens my counsel
with words without knowledge?
Job 38:2

His name is Michael Campareri. He's nine years old. He also happens to be the U.S. National Chess Champion. At the tender age of three, his parents discovered he liked to play chess and seemed pretty good at it too. So they bought him a computer chess game. He mastered it. At the age of six, they got a chess coach for him, but the coach soon quit. His ego was bruised when Michael consistently beat him. Today, people of all ages who think they are pretty good at the game get trounced on a regular basis by this young champ.

Recently, he took on some twenty young chess players, moving from board to board, quickly knocking them out of the game. "He kills you on the opening move, then he kills you again," said one of them. They described him as professional, focused and exacting.[6]

And by the way, there is one more thing you need to know about Michael. He has been diagnosed with ADD!

Dr. Kathi J. Kemper, a holistic pediatrician, says that if your child has been diagnosed with ADD (Attention Deficit Disorder) there are several things you need to know. There are changes you can make in your lifestyle and eating habits that can make a big difference. She would also be quick to tell you: Not every child diagnosed with ADD (perhaps like Michael) has a problem that needs to be medicated.

Doctors who practice general medicine are trained to see a problem and eliminate it. But doctors who practice holistic medicine attempt to treat the whole person. Dr. Kemper feels strongly that kids need to know they are not bad

Not every child diagnosed with ADD has a problem that needs to be medicated.

simply because they have trouble paying attention. She would quickly tell you that perhaps it is you as a parent who needs help—not your child.[7]

In evaluating what is happening to our children today, I go back to Scripture and ask myself, Did Elijah also have ADD? Was it possible that John the Baptist—antisocial, living in isolation with a diet of locusts and wild honey—could have been diagnosed as having a bipolar disorder? Was Judas suffering from acute depression? Is there nothing in Scripture to which we can relate our problems today?

INSIGHT

The title of this selection says it all: The diagnosis may be wrong!

There is and there isn't. I'm convinced that our lifestyle today has produced all kinds of situations which were never God's intention. Elijah, the twelve apostles who walked with Jesus, those we read about in the New Testament never watched TV nor played a computer game. For the most part they were outdoors. They lived outdoors, they walked, they exercised and they breathed fresh air.

Of course there is no going back. But this truth has never changed: God cares. He cares infinitely about you, your child and your well-being. He's there to give you direction and help when you need it.

THINK ON THIS

1   If your child really does need Ritalin or another medication, don't feel guilty.

2   Help your youngster know that he is
not naughty or bad when it is
impossible for him to sit still.

RESOURCE READING

Job 42

THE BALANCING ACT
OF PARENTING

I tell you the truth, anyone who will not
receive the kingdom of God
like a little child will never enter it.
Mark 10:15

The young mother yelled at her child, "Be quiet!" A look at the child—barely a year old—told me that the child was sick. The mother's nerves were on edge. Her older children had colds too. But the little child couldn't turn off the tears anymore readily than I could sing in Swedish or grow hair on the top of my head now that it has disappeared. What the child did understand though, was the tone of voice—the message was negative, very negative.

I didn't say anything, but I began to reflect on the fact that parenting is a constant struggle to maintain balance.

Observation 1: The wise parent has to balance expectations with abilities.
Obviously, the ability of the sick child to stop crying was beyond the mother's expectations. It was

impossible, period. Punishing a child for what he is incapable of doing is not only wrong but also counterproductive.

"But your older sister can do math! Why can't you?" The fact is that every child is different. Just because an older child can do something doesn't necessarily mean that another child can do the same task at the same age.

Observation 2: The wise parent has to balance love and discipline.

You can discipline a child without love but you cannot love a child without discipline. Disciplining is one way of saying, "I love you too much to let you get away with this (talking back to me, throwing your food all over the table, sticking your tongue out at the teacher)."

Parenting is an ongoing process of balancing expectations with reality.

Does the Bible make a case for discipline? Yes, a strong one. Does it make as strong a case for loving your child? Absolutely. Both are important and both must be balanced.

Observation 3: The wise parent has to balance protecting a child from hard knocks and letting him experience the consequences of his actions.

This especially applies to older children. Do you lie for your teenager to protect him, or let him face the court when he's been drinking? I'm convinced that parents do their child a disservice when they fail to help him understand that with every choice there are consequences, sometimes tough ones.

Observation 4: Successful parenting has to balance turning loose with holding on.

> **INSIGHT**
>
> *Parenting is bringing out the best in our children without condemning them for what they cannot do or making them feel inadequate when they fail to meet our expectations.*

Two mistakes of parenting are being overly strict and being overly permissive. Turn a child loose too soon, give him too much independence, and he will get into trouble, but hold on to the youngster for too long and he's certain to become angry and rebellious.

THINK ON THIS

When facing a tough decision about your children, talk the situation over with an older, more mature friend—a parent, an older person in your church, or a neighbor you respect. Sometimes hearing someone else tell you what you already know in your heart is affirming and encouraging.

RESOURCE READING

Proverbs 22

WHEN CHILDREN BECOME OUR VICTIMS

An angry man stirs up dissension, and a
hot-tempered one commits many sins.
Proverbs 29:22

Is there more child abuse today, or is it simply that we are hearing more about it?" That was the question I asked a psychologist who also happens to be an ordained minister. Dr. Millard Sall believes that there is more child abuse today than a generation ago, and we are hearing more about it.

For a long while some teachers, school administrators and even the police refused to get involved in domestic affairs because they felt that what takes place between a parent and a child is personal. They knew there were some parents who were out of control and took out their anger on their children. But child abuse is a subject that bears a social stigma. And so for a long while our indifference scarred the future of thousands of victims.

How much child abuse is there? Only God knows for sure. Estimates in the US are in the millions and some feel that the actual number of children who are physically abused in the course of a year is closer to 10 million, depending on how abuse is defined. Child abuse is a universal problem, yet many incidents go unreported and unnoticed. Unnoticed, that is, save by the victims who will bear emotional and/or physical scars for the rest of their lives.

Another question I put to Dr. Sall is this: "Just what is child abuse?" Dr. Sall says that physical child abuse is not discipline. A willfully

We've got to learn how to manage our anger and frustration and not take them out on our children.

disobedient or defiant child can be physically disciplined without drawing blood, causing welts or injuring a child's spirit. The purpose of discipline is to enforce proper behavior, but punishment is abusive and can greatly harm a child.

Children become victims of abuse every year. Their physical injuries include burns on tiny hands placed on a stove or made by cigarette butts, knife wounds, dislocations and fractures, and sexual abuse, which is a whole subject in itself. The emotional trauma can scar a person for life.

I, for one, will never forget the shock I felt when I went to the Los Angeles County morgue and saw firsthand the horrible results of child abuse. It isn't even fit to write about it but it is taking place in our out-of-control society today.

Why are so many innocent children becoming victims today? Healthcare workers who are involved with children generally point out three basic reasons:

1   Some parents with emotional problems such as low self-esteem, volatile temper or a marked lack of patience and self-control will take out their frustrations on those closest in proximity—often their own helpless children.

2   Certain children tend to bring out the worst in their parents. For example, children who are hyperactive by nature go non-stop from their waking moment until they drop exhausted. Stress continues to mount as a parent despairs of speaking calmly or rationally.

3   Marital stress, which ranges from financial pressures to broken homes, also creates distress and some of that is transferred to children.

In simple terms, often parents can't cope, and as a result their children become victims. A sad legacy of child abuse is that victims face a greater chance of growing up duplicating this act of aggression on their own children. "All right," you may be thinking to yourself, "The problem exists. What can be done about it?"

First, we need to recognize it is everybody's problem. Ignoring the issue only aggravates the situation. When a child has bruises or welts, black eyes or injuries, someone needs to be held accountable, and our failure to do so not only is a grave injustice to the child but also abets violence.

Second, we adults facing stress and pressure must learn how to cope. This requires emotional ventilation through exercise—hard, vigorous exercise; prayer and therapy; and facing the issue clearly. Almost every person knows where his boiling point is, and if you feel that you are losing control, you have to get help.

We can't blame our society, however wrong it is. We must accept responsibility for our own actions.

INSIGHT

There is a limit to what you can handle. When you feel that you are being pushed to breaking point, you need to get help for yourself lest your children become victims.

THINK ON THIS

1 Don't discipline your child when you are angry even though he has done wrong. It's unfair to your child and also dangerous.

2 If you were a victim of violence when you were growing up, you have a greater tendency to be violent than the person who had not experienced this as a child.

3 If you—even once—have inappropriately struck, hit or kicked your child, you need professional help. Realizing this and admitting it is the first step.

RESOURCE READING

Proverbs 29

CHRISTIAN VALUES 101

*Fathers, do not exasperate your children;
instead, bring them up in the training and
instruction of the Lord.*
Ephesians 6:4

O ne father thought that he knew the
formula for conveying values to children.
He told the press that he really believed
a child would turn out just fine if the parents
loved the child, spent plenty of time with him,
involved him in wholesome activities and helped
him get a balanced education. He said,
"Suddenly after seventeen years of dedicated
effort, something happened to my foolproof
plan. I found I was the father of a murderer."

What happened? The son was sentenced to
twenty-five years in prison after pleading guilty to
the murder of his 16-year-old girlfriend who had
spurned his advances. The father said, "The shock,
the agony and soul-searching are unbelievable.

Everything you believe in is gone in one bolt of lightning that rips your heart. What went wrong? Nothing fits your notions of criminal behavior and what to do about it."

No parent dares be so smug or sure of himself that he can take lightly what this brokenhearted dad told the press. But the question remains, "What went wrong? What caused the son to turn his back on everything his parents believed in?"

Of one thing you can be certain. Every parent, no matter what he does, conveys a value system to his child—be it a positive value system or one that allows the child to do whatever he pleases.

The greatest influence on a child's value system is his mother and father, at least in the long term. In the short term, it could be his peer group. A child's value system becomes a reflection of the aggregate

Taking time for hobbies, for recreation, for worship, for time together is all part of showing your child what you think is important.

influences in his life, whether they are what he sees on TV and the media, what friends think or the impact that church and God have made in his life. A parent who models the message and reflects the kind of value system in his personal life that he wants his child to embrace is far more effective that a parent who talks about one thing but practices another.

The parent who acknowledges personal failure when it happens is also teaching an important lesson: As we confess our sin and failure, our heavenly Father forgives us and gives us the strength to overcome. But the parent who pretends to be perfect when in reality he is fallible is teaching hypocrisy. Kids pick up on that very quickly.

No parent, however, can convey much of a value system when he is not there. Taking time for hobbies, for recreation, for worship, for time together is all part of showing your child what you think is important. Don't for a moment confuse quality time with quantity time. They aren't the same, and no stretch of the imagination can convince you that a couple of hours on the weekend can compensate for your absence Monday through Friday.

INSIGHT

To have an accurate "read" on where your teenager is mentally, emotionally and spiritually, you've got to be there with him—and not to know only that he's in his room, door closed, earphones blaring music (the words of which you have never heard). Time spent one-on-one is the only way to get a feel for what's happening to your child.

Out of the tragedy of the shooting at Columbine High School in Littletown, Colorado in 1999 came the realization that the two young men who so callously took the lives of their classmates were living in a world totally divorced from the one their parents thought they were in. The parents simply were not aware of what their children were thinking, of what was influencing them and how they felt about issues of major importance. Their assumptions were 180 degrees opposite reality.

Every child has a will of his own. Regardless of that, most parents still feel personal failure when a child goes wrong. Follow the biblical mandate of raising your child in the discipline and the instruction of the Lord, and then let God do His work in your child's heart. You can trust Him to do His part when you have done yours. He can work in a heart where no one else can.

THINK ON THIS

1   Plan a one-on-one time with your youngster. How about a lunch or breakfast date with your daughter? A backpacking or a basketball game with your son? A hobby or work project?

2   Take your planner and note exactly how
    much time you spent with your son or
    daughter in the last three months. Now
    compare that with the time spent with
    your friends.

RESOURCE READING

2 Peter 1:3-22

TEACHING HONESTY TO YOUR CHILDREN

*But mark this: There will be terrible times
in the last days. People will be lovers of themselves, lovers of
money, boastful, proud, abusive, disobedient to their
parents, ungrateful, unholy, without love, unforgiving,
slanderous, without self-control, brutal, not lovers of the
good, treacherous, rash, conceited, lovers of pleasure rather
than lovers of God—having a form of godliness but denying
its power. Have nothing to do with them.*
2 Timothy 3:1-5

Children lie for the same reasons that adults lie: To avoid punishment, to win respect, to appear better than they are, or to feel safe because they feel threatened. Without realizing it, many parents teach their children to lie and actually encourage them in the practice.

Want to teach the importance of honesty to your child?

1 Model honesty yourself.

Children who often lie have parents who lie, and very quickly youngsters learn from their parents' example. They overhear Mom saying on the phone, "No, John isn't at home" when Dad is parked in front of the TV and doesn't want to be disturbed. They pick up on phony excuses you make; they hear you lying to the traffic officer who has caught you driving without a license.

2 Be honest with your child.

When your kids are faced with a problem, don't expect them to respond with honesty if you aren't honest with them. For example, you have lost your job and you stay at home. But you explain away the whole situation, thinking that you are sparing the child the anguish of knowing you are without work. Your children can sense your

Without realizing it, many parents teach their children to lie and actually encourage them in the practice.

stress and insecurity, although they do not know what is happening. This can do more damage than telling the truth.

Here is another example: Your child's grandmother had a stroke and is hospitalized. Telling your child that everything is all right when he has seen the pain in the family will confuse him. Better to explain that Grandma is very sick and take this as an opportunity to point out that we can trust God in difficult situations.

3 Don't give your youngster an opportunity to lie; rather, make it easy for him to tell the truth.

Suppose you have laid down certain geographic boundaries and you expect your child to stay within them. But you know for a fact that your child didn't stay within them. Don't ask, "Did you go beyond the corner at the end of the block?" Instead ask, "Why did you go into the next block?" It gives your child a reason to explain his behavior rather than to deny his actions.

However, when parents are overly restrictive, they set the stage for dishonesty. Far better is open and free communication so your child has the freedom to say, "I don't think that you are being fair in what you are doing." That can be done without malice or anger. Open communication evaluates the situation and allows a youngster to express himself without talking back disrespectfully.

> **INSIGHT**
>
> *Children can learn to be dishonest out of fear for the consequences of their actions or by following the example of others. Make sure you model the message of absolute honesty that you want your child to embrace.*

4 Stress the fact that what others may do is different from what you do in your family.

Very early in life children begin to understand what truth is. Child psychologists say that by age four most children can sift fantasy from truth. If they have playmates who make it a practice to lie, you must teach your children that honesty is a fundamental matter of trust and love in your family. Help them to understand that when trust is lost, relationships are affected. If the wrong behavior of other kids begins to influence them, put those kids off limits to your child. When your child learns that you still love and accept him when he has behaved unacceptably, it helps him to be honest with you, regardless of the consequences.

Honesty is the best policy—it's the only way to build relationships that endure.

THINK ON THIS

Before you blame others for influencing your child negatively, ask yourself, "Do I ever have people say, 'No, he's not here' on the telephone when I don't want to talk? Do I bend the truth myself?" Be honest. Here's where you need to begin applying the straight ruler of truth.

RESOURCE READING

Acts 5:1-10

YOUR EXAMPLE

*Therefore everyone who hears
these words of mine and puts them into
practice is like a wise man who
built his house on the rock.*
Matthew 7:24

Several theologians were discussing the merits of different modern Bible translations. Each one seemed to have a favorite and offered several good reasons why his choice was superior to other versions. "King James is archaic," one contended. Another believed that the New International Version takes too much liberty with the text in trying to be relevant.

Overhearing the conversation, another man spoke, "Frankly, I liked my father's translation."

"Oh, did your father translate the New Testament?" asked one of the men, who knew that the man's father was quite a scholar.

"Yes," he replied. "He translated it into his life, and that's why I'm serving the Lord today!"

The best translation of the Bible is that which is

lived out by our examples day by day as we face the realities of living in a broken, sinful world. In recent days we have lamented the moral collapse of our world, often blaming "the system." We denounce secularism, the New Age movement, the moral breakdown of society. Of course, all of these do impact the world and the educational system where our children spend considerable time.

Yet these forces, sinister and diabolical as they may be, are not destroying our children as much as our failure to teach right from wrong and to convey the old-fashioned, God-given values to them. I'm thinking of a college girl who wrote and said, "My mother objects to my living with my boyfriend, yet she spends weekends with her new boyfriend. So what's the difference?"

Values are formed by the environment in which children grow up, including the attitudes and actions of parents.

Values are formed by the environment in which children grow up, including the attitudes and actions of parents. When you live like a devil, you can't expect your children to walk like saints. Recently I heard a child about three years of age using profanity which I am certain the child couldn't comprehend at all. His language was what he heard at home.

No parent chooses the period in which he raises his children. Being a parent now includes living within the parameters of the world in which we live. Have you ever considered that those who lived during the time of the early Church, including the disciples who walked with Jesus, didn't have a very easy time in raising their children either? But you can choose how to respond to the needs of your children, thus expressing your value system. When you hug them and show affection, they know they are loved. When you take time to read with them, they grow intellectually. When you pray and read Bible stories to them, you teach right from wrong. When you live out a code of morality and honesty, your children learn commitment and integrity in marriage. When you show respect to elderly parents and law enforcement officials, your children show respect to you. When you attend church and take your

> ## INSIGHT
>
> *Your kids don't expect perfection from you but they do want authenticity. Hearing you say, "I'm sorry for what I did; I was a lousy example for you" teaches an important lesson: Christians are not perfect, just forgiven. As God forgives us, so we must ask for and extend forgiveness to others.*

children, you show them what is important to you. When you discuss issues and pray about them together as a family, you are showing that disagreements can be solved without hostility and violence.

There is a place for dissent. There is a time for anger. There are causes that must be defended. There are wrongs that cannot be ignored and must be fought, but all these are no substitute for the presence of parents who assume the God-given responsibility of raising a child.

Our children are God's way of saying, "There is hope for the future!" They are our great responsibility.

THINK ON THIS

1 When you are wrong, admit it. Bluffing your way through a situation when everyone knows you are wrong only angers and frustrates your children.
2 Strive to be the message you want your kids to see and hear.

RESOURCE READING

2 Corinthians 3:1-5

YOUR INFLUENCE VS. THE INFLUENCE OF CULTURE

For I have chosen him, so that he will direct his children and his household after him to keep the way of the LORD by doing what is right and just, so that the LORD will bring about for Abraham what he has promised him.
Genesis 18:19

When Judith Rich Harris's book *The Nurture Assumption* was published in 1999, thousands of professionals said she didn't know what she was talking about. Harris contended that it is other kids—not parents—who are influencing teenagers today.[8]

I am convinced that many parents today think they are the major influence in their kids' lives when in reality, they provide only a roof over their kids' heads, food on the table and enough spending money to allow the youngsters to indulge in anything they want—junk food, junk music, junk entertainment and junk friends. Then when a disaster occurs, they cry out, "God, how could this have happened? I've given my children everything money could buy."

What they are missing is the very essence of parental involvement—a spiritual connection and, communication that is more than, "So you need more money, huh? What did you do with what I just gave you?"

Lynda Madison is a clinical psychologist who works with teens, many of whom have been suicidal. She is convinced that parents think they are communicating with their teens when in reality both parents and children tell each other what they think the other wants to hear. A mother says, "How did your day go?" The teenage daughter rolls her eyes—which her mother doesn't see—and replies, "Oh, just fine" as she retreats to her room to call a friend.

Many parents today think they are the major influence in the lives of their kids, when in reality, they provide only material things.

Madison also believes that teens and their parents would like to know what's going on in each other's lives without really getting involved. Polite, meaningless exchanges of trivia become the substitutes of really knowing, deeply caring and being there for each other.

Family First, an independent, nonprofit research and communications organization, has done extensive research among both parents and teens, exploring the relationship between parents—or the absence of them—and teenage violence today. Their most recent report says,

"When asked to identify the leading cause of youth violence... adults and teens disagree. One-third of adults (34%) cite 'divorce and fathers who are not involved in their kids' lives,' as the leading cause of youth violence, followed by 'violence on TV, in movies, in music and on the Internet' (21%) and 'teen drug use' (20%).

Teens have slightly different views about the cause of youth violence. One-third (31%) of teens say 'teen drug use' is the primary cause of youth violence followed by 'access to weapons' (26%) and 'violence on TV, in movies, in music and on the Internet' (21%). Significantly fewer teens than adults (11% versus 34% respectively) point to 'divorce and fathers who are not involved in kids' lives' as the leading cause of youth violence."⁹

INSIGHT

Statistics are not iron-clad, self-fulfilling prophecies as to how your child will go.

Yes, I understand that you can lead a horse to water but you can't make it drink. Yes, I concur that there are times when a parent is there for his kids in school, in church, and at home as well, yet the youth still turns his back on God and chooses to go the wrong way.

But I also know that for generations, parents have proved what the Bible said long ago, that when parents teach and train a child in the way he should go, setting the example in their personal lives, that youngster treads in their footsteps. It may just take a while.

THINK ON THIS

1   Since a child follows in the footsteps of a parent, it's wise to ask where you yourself are headed.
2   It is possible that your youngster is living in an entirely different world than you think. He may say, "Yes, Dad!" or "Sure, Mom," telling you what he thinks you want to hear but doesn't really mean it. Do you care to find out?

RESOURCE READING
Matthew 18:1-5

WHERE DID MY KID LEARN THIS?

Be very careful, then, how you live—not as unwise but as wise, making the most of every opportunity, because the days are evil.
Ephesians 5:15-16

"Dear Dr. Sala," writes a friend of *Guidelines,* "I found an [audio] tape where my eleven-year-old used vulgar language including the 'F' word. Also, I was called by the principal of my thirteen-year-old's school and was told that he put up his middle finger at his teacher. We are supposed to be Christians, and I wonder where my children learned all these things."

More than one parent had asked, "What's gone wrong? Where have I failed?"

It's a fact that parenting is not an easy task. It's tough to get the job done, yet quite often parental failure happens. The sad thing is that so many parents assume they are imparting values when in reality they are allowing the values of the world to shape the lives of their children. Then they throw up their hands in dismay and say, "I can't understand what's happened!"

Let's take a look at some of the most powerful forces at work in the lives of our children and see what kind of influences they make.

What's the greatest force in the lives of children today? I don't think anyone would challenge me if I say, "the media." John Condry of Cornell University contends that the average child in America now spends one-third of his waking hours watching TV or playing video games.

In answering the question, "Where are my children learning values?" better take a hard look at the number of hours they sit in front of the TV or a computer with unsupervised access to the Internet.

It's easy to blame the media, our children's friends and the educational system for our children's poor behavior when the real cause is our own parental failure.

The second most influential factor in the life of a child is his peer group, which includes his schoolmates. Here the possible influence of a parent is lost by default. In many homes, children are spending some period in their lives living with only one parent. Often, due to the parent's long working hours, children are left to themselves much of the time. Friends become their major influence. An empty house, unsupervised activities and boredom combine to bring out the worst in a child striving to find approval and support from his peers.

The third influence is school. School was once a place where a child could receive positive moral and social input, but today many teachers strive just to make it through the day. Sometimes a teacher will even use profanity—but let a teacher in the US talk about God or the Ten Commandments, and he's subject to reproof and censure. Kids become streetwise but lack sound moral instruction.

> ### Insight
>
> *Our kids are much more "streetwise" than we were at their age, and subsequently more sophisticated. Helping them think for themselves—as opposed to going with the flow of their peer group—is a positive step forward.*

What about the influence of a parent's life? It's easy to blame the media, our children's friends and the educational system for our children's poor behavior when the real cause is parental failure, our own failure. I understand that not working may not be an option, but feeling guilty because you need to have a job only compounds the problem. It's much better to be alert: Use the phone to check on them, ask who is in the house, what homework has to be done, what's going on.

Before you ask, "How did this happen?" when your kids get in trouble, better take stock now and act. It's your responsibility as a parent.

THINK ON THIS

When moral situations confront your family, rather than simply condemning the person who failed, talk about how the situation could have been better handled. Ask, "Is there anything we could have done differently?"

RESOURCE READING

1 Corinthians 6:9-20

CONVEYING VALUES TO YOUR CHILDREN

Know therefore that the LORD your God is
God; he is the faithful God, keeping his
covenant of love to a thousand generations
of those who love him and keep his commands.
Deuteronomy 7:9

Interested in conveying a positive value system to your child? First, you and your spouse need to be on the same wavelength. Talk about what values are important to both of you.

Next, take a look at your environment. What surrounds your child? What are the influences in his life—television, friends, magazines? (By the way, your kid knows everything that goes on in your life. He reads you better than you read him. He knows what's in the bottom drawer of your cabinet as well as the top shelf in your closet.)

Then, evaluate the people who influence your child. Who are they? Next to you as a parent, who would you say has the greatest influence in your child's life? A babysitter? The boy down the street? The neighbor's children who watch TV with your child before you come home from work? Would you include grandparents?

It is amazing what a great influence your extended family can have in the lives of your children. And they have to be there. They have to be willing to invest the time. I'm not suggesting they do the "heavy work" of parenting, but they can reinforce, encourage and be a friend.

The next step is to evaluate what positive biblical teaching and Christian values you are conveying. TV has never had a greater negative impact than today, but to balance that out, never

Negatively or positively, the most profound impact in any child's life is the example of Mom and Dad.

before has there been so much good, positive stuff available. I'm thinking of Christian videos and tapes which kids can quickly memorize.

Are you in church on a regular basis? Do you go beyond that, sharing the Bible with your family through family devotions and bedtime stories? If not, why not? No church—no matter how great— can substitute for what you can do at home. How about holding a regular weekly Bible Study in your house? Some of your kids' friends could attend too.

What about your influence in your child's life? Negatively or positively, the most profound impact in any child's life is the example of Mom and Dad. Some, in fact, believe that the father's influence, which may not even be as intimate and personal, is even greater than a mother's when it comes to shaping a child's outlook.

"Daddy," a little boy of about six asked as his mother was preparing to take him to Sunday school, "how old do I have to be before I can stay home with you and read the comics?" Enough said.

> ### INSIGHT
>
> *Lacking the maturity that you have as an adult, your child can't handle some things that you can. That's why you need to put some things aside or give them up—a minor sacrifice for the sake of your child.*

Being a parent is an awesome responsibility. But it is one of the greatest experiences of life, and it can be one of the most rewarding. You can have it that way. It can still be done.

THINK ON THIS

Ponder what the *Insight* on this page might mean to your family.

RESOURCE READING
1 Kings 13

YOUR CHILDREN ARE
WORTH FIGHTING FOR!

*Don't be misled; remember that you can't
ignore God and get away with it; a man will
always reap just the kind of crop he sows!
Galatians 6:7, TLB*

What kind of kids are we going to have in another generation?" asked a concerned parent and educator as he reflected on the number of children today growing up in one-parent homes. These kids' role models are movie stars and heroes who tend to settle scores with violence rather than negotiation.

Do you ever think much about what the world will be like in the next generation, especially if lifestyle trends which began in the 60s and the 70s continue? If the foundation is destroyed, what hope is there for the house?

An old story is told about a young marine who was carrying the radio when his unit was pinned down by hostile fire. Quickly, he contacted headquarters and was asked what the situation was. He replied, "The enemy is to the north and south, the east and west. Actually," he replied excitedly, "we're surrounded by 'em."

"Well," said the sergeant at headquarters, "What do you think?"

The young man swallowed hard as he replied, "Well, sir, the enemy won't get away from us now!"

That's the way it will be raising children in a hostile world. What can we do to help insure that our kids can make it no matter what the shape of the world of the twenty-first century will be? There's plenty you can do. Fight back with these powerful guidelines:

1 Teach your child to be his own person.
Help him understand that it's OK to be different, to say no, to resist the pressure to conform. If you can win in this, you have passed on to your child a tremendous tool in fighting negative influences in the future. Today, peer pressure is one of the most powerful

> *Help your children understand that it's OK to be different, to say no, to resist the pressure to conform.*

forces confronting children and teenagers. How do you teach a child that it's OK not to go along with the crowd? You've got to be secure yourself and at peace with your life. Family loyalty and commitment to each other is part of that answer.

2 Teach your child how to manage anger.

"Be angry and do not sin," (Ephesians 4:26, *NKJV*) is the biblical admonition. This requires both the example of a parent and the patience of a teacher.

Note that I didn't say make your child understand that all anger is wrong. Managing anger means learning to direct our anger toward situations that are wrong, not at people who challenge us. Angry adults transfer their emotions to children, who in turn take out their hostilities on each other. Nobody gets his way all the time, and the person who lets a child get away with whatever he wants is not helping that child come to grips with the real world.

> **INSIGHT**
> *You, as a parent, are the answer to the question, "What kind of kids are we going to have in another generation?" Your lifestyle becomes the message.*

3 Teach your child that there are consequences to every choice and action.

Our choices determine the consequences. It's the cause-and-effect relation in life. If you choose to cheat, the consequences may be flunking the test. When a child chooses disobedience, and he knows that the consequence will be discipline, that child also learns that life rewards or punishes us the same way. The undesirable consequences come with the choice.

This is the way life is, and in a real sense, the parent who fails to teach his child that every choice produces consequences shortchanges him. Then when he gets out in the real world and discovers that he doesn't study and flunks, or he doesn't attend his classes and gets expelled, he thinks that the world is unfair. The eternal law of the harvest is that "a man reaps what he sows" (Galatians 6:7).

4 Teach your child that problems can be solved.
There is a solution to every problem. Life is full of challenges and difficulties which can be met.

5 Give your child a value system that distinguishes right from wrong—and chooses the right.
You'll be glad you did. Your kids are worth fighting for!

THINK ON THIS

1 If you lie for your child to save him from discipline at school, what message does this convey to your child? To others regarding your character?

2 Keeping communication lively and
   vibrant is important. How do you do
   this? Can you separate censure from
   openness?

RESOURCE READING
Psalm 103

PROTECTING YOUR CHILD FROM SEXUAL PREDATORS

*Be on guard! Be alert! You do not know when
that time will come. It's like a man going
away: He leaves his house and puts his
servants in charge, each with his assigned task,
and tells the one at the door to keep watch.*
Mark 13:33-34

As we drove past the elementary school, we
noticed the long line of cars waiting to pick
up the children who were finishing their
school day. "Boy," I commented—half speaking to
my wife and half to myself—"things sure are
different when our kids went to school." A generation
ago, perhaps even a decade ago, few parents felt
concern when kids walked home. After all, there
were neighbors and it was generally safe.

Today, it's a different world. Sexual predators
know where to find your kids. A youngster with a
lunch box or a backpack walking by himself
becomes an unsuspecting target, a potential victim.
Dangers far more deadly than nerve gas or
chemical warfare lurk out there as predators target
our children with sexual violence.

How do you protect your child from sexual predators? How do you warn your kids that not everybody can be trusted while you emphasize family solidarity and respect for elders? It's not easy, but if you don't teach your child to be alert and perceptive, it can be the gravest mistake you can ever make. In some cases, a parent's negligence can be fatal; in others, a parent's failure can result in emotional scars in a child that would be there for life.

Step 1: Know who could take advantage of your child.

The most likely predator is not the notorious convict who has just been released from prison. It's someone you and probably your child already know. The fact is that eighty percent of all sexual predators are acquaintances or friends of the family or relatives. That fact in itself

If you simply choose to look the other way in your embarrassment, you contribute to ongoing abuse.

disarms the youngster, who reasons, "How could this nice person—Daddy's friend, Uncle Paul or Grandpa—do something bad?" He's apt to be a nice guy: a stepdad, a distant relative, a scoutmaster who likes sleepovers with the boys or—sad as it is—the youth pastor or the parish priest.

Step 2: Educate, teach, instruct.

Make sure your child knows what's proper and improper. That it's not OK for a family member or a close friend to touch any part of the body that would be covered by a swimsuit.

Step 3: Be perceptive without being paranoid.

This is for both you and your child. Many children become victims when a stranger asks for help, or when someone shows up and says, "Your mom wants me to take you home," when usually it is you who picks up your child. In a non-frightening but firm manner, you must teach your youngster that if someone tries to grab him, he should bite, yell and scream, and run—but he should never go with the stranger.

> INSIGHT
>
> *Our hesitance to talk about sex or to prepare our children for emergencies helps make it easy for sexual predators to take advantage of them.*

Step 4: Know the symptoms of abuse.

In an article entitled, "Sudden Mood Swings Called Clues to Abuse," Carolyn Poirot, a writer for the *Fort Worth Star-Telegram*, says, "If children have been sexually abused outside the home, they may not want to go to school or the day care center and may cry and cling to mother. Or they regress.[10]

Step 5: Never give anyone a second chance.
Forgiveness is not the issue; the safety of your child is. In all probability your youngster is not the sexual predator's first victim. If you simply choose to look the other way out of embarrassment, you contribute to ongoing abuse.

Step 6: Always believe your child when he tells you about inappropriate activity.
Your child has no cause to deceive you. Children rarely lie about these matters.

Step 7: Realize there is healing and help if you have been a victim.
If you were a victim long ago, there is healing and help. But God forbid that by indifference or neglect we should make it easy for anyone to be a sexual predator.

THINK ON THIS

1   Make sure your children know they should tell you if someone takes advantage of them.
2   Work out a backup plan—if they fail to ride in their schoolbus, or if you're picking them up and you're delayed in traffic, or if you should go home from

the office sick and couldn't pick them up,
they should know what to do.

3   Be alert. Don't be too trusting in regard
to your child even with people you think
you know very well.

RESOURCE READING

2 Timothy 3:1-9

WINNING THE BATTLE
OVER VALUES

Eli asked, "What happened, my son?"
1 Samuel 4:16

Parenting is one of the scariest things that a person ever does. Walk a tightrope over Niagara Falls, free-fall out of an airplane, climb Mt. Apo or hang-glide over Tokyo and you'll probably survive. But in this business of parenting you cannot afford to take risks. It comes with no guarantees; there is no customer service center where you can exchange a kid and start over.

Even Christian leaders—godly men and women— can be failures when it comes to raising children.

There are parents like Jonathan Edwards, whose godly descendents number among the hundreds, including Christian doctors, lawyers, judges and educators. Then there are those like Hannah Whitall Smith, a godly woman and author, whose children all turned their backs on God and Christian values. If someone like that was a failure as a parent, we think, then how can I succeed as a parent in today's world of drugs, promiscuity and tremendous peer pressure? I'm glad you asked, because today's guidelines answer that very issue.

What can parents do to win at parenting?

Guideline1: Keep your relationship with God and your spouse right.

Nothing is more important than standing together spiritually as a husband and wife. Remember, values are caught, not taught. When two parents love each other, support each other, pray together and go to church together, they have a hedge against future failure. Does this mean that a single parent can't raise godly children? No. But, when one parent teaches one set of values, and the other teaches the opposite, the challenge of successful parenting is far greater.

You are your child's most effective teacher.

Guideline 2: Protect your child's environment.

A farmer was talking about raising chickens when he said, "You don't put live chicks under a dead hen." Neither do you expose your child to spiritually devastating influences and expect them to come through unscathed. Christian parents need to take seriously what the Scripture teaches that we are in the world but not of the world.

The battle lines are drawn today, and to ignore that fact exposes your child to a host of influences that will leave their mark on his life and soul. At some point you've got to be willing to draw the line and say, "This is far enough, and not an inch farther."

Environment includes what comes into your home through television, what your children learn in the classroom, your children's friends. A whole gamut of important issues are raised: Should I put my children in private school, home school or public school? There are no easy answers, but the issue of environment must be faced.

Guideline 3: Teach your child to evaluate what he hears and sees, and to think for himself.

I have become absolutely convinced recently that teaching a child to think through cause-and-effect relationships give him the strength to say, "No way! I choose to be my own person."

Guideline 4: Model the message yourself.
You are your child's most effective teacher. "Do not be deceived: God cannot be mocked," says Paul. "A man reaps what he sows. The one who sows to please his sinful nature, from that nature will reap destruction; the one who sows to please the Spirit, from the Spirit will reap eternal life" (Galatians 6:7-8). That is also true of parenting.

THINK ON THIS

1   Peer pressure can be lessened by introducing your child to new friends who have the same set of values as you and are committed to what you believe is important. Where do you find them? In your church? In your family and among the children of your close friends?

2   Two extremes are wrong—being too strict (withdrawn and separated from what you feel is wrong) and being too permissive (anything goes). Where do you find yourself? How do you find the balance?

3   When you and your mate disagree, how do you handle it?

RESOURCE READING
1 Samuel 4

PASSING THE BATON

*So now, if the boy is not with us when I
go back to your servant my father and if
my father, whose life is closely bound up
with the boy's life, sees that the
boy isn't there, he will die.*
Genesis 44:30-31

Almost every Olympics brings new world
records and a new class of hero-athletes.
The margin of success is often so narrow—
even a fraction of a second—that one slight mistake
can mean disaster.

In the relay events, an athlete must run
alongside the next runner and slap the baton into
his open hand. Then he accelerates and runs until it
is his turn to pass on the baton to the next person.

In the Summer Olympics of 1996, one national
relay team was expected to win or at least place
among the medallists, but their hopes were dashed
when the lead runner reached for the open hand of
his successor, who grasped the baton, then dropped
it. By the time he had recovered the baton, the
race was history and his team had lost. I remember
watching Zola Budd running barefoot in the

Olympics of 1984 when Mary Decker tripped over her and both stumbled badly.

Frankly, I like to win. Of course, winning isn't everything, but there is no thrill comparable to being the first to break the tape or to come in ahead of your competitor, even if it is by a hair. I'm the same way when it comes to parenting. No parent who really loves his children wants to see a single one stumble and fall.

How does a parent pass on the baton of faith, slapping it into the hands of the next generation, who will grasp it and impart the same value system that they received growing up? Those who do succeed have a reward far greater than standing on the winner's pedestal and having a gold medal placed around their neck.

If you want to raise a winner, then preach less and practice more.

You can't pass on the baton of faith to your offspring unless you have it firmly in your grasp. That's where a lot of parents fail. You can lecture your kid on right and wrong until you strain your vocal chords, but it is a waste of breath unless you live it out before him. If you want to raise a winner, then preach less and practice more.

To hand on to your child a lively and strong faith in God, a knowledge of right and wrong, and an understanding of fairness and compassion is to place the baton of faith firmly in his grasp. Your child may stumble, but chances are he will never let go of what you have given him.

Model the value system that you believe is important.
Winning is important, but winning isn't as important as striving fairly and honestly. Ben Johnson, known as "the human bullet," and often described as "the fastest man alive," learned this the hard way. Though he won his event, he was later disqualified for taking steroids in the Summer Olympics of 1988. Surrendering his medal with disgrace, he returned to his homeland Canada a humbled man.

> **INSIGHT**
>
> *Every parent, no matter what he does—either negatively or positively—is conveying a message to his child regarding values, regarding right and wrong, regarding God and our world.*

Be there when your child needs your help.
Who will forget that scene in the Summer Olympics of 1992, of a father whose son had pulled a hamstring? The father ran to the track and put his arms under his son, and the two of them limped toward the finish line. While most of us have forgotten the athlete's name, none who saw it will ever forget the emotional impact of a father who was there for his child.

Love them unconditionally and keep the lines of communication open.

As a dad doesn't reject his little boy who stumbles and falls learning to walk, a wise father doesn't disown the teenage son who is learning through failure.

Someone once said that your children are the only thing you can take to heaven with you. As Judah put it long ago, "How shall I go up to my father if the lad is not with me?" (Genesis 44:34, NKJV) Yes, how?

THINK ON THIS

1   If you can't give your children faith because you don't have it yourself, get down on your knees and ask God to forgive you, to give you strength to live for Him and to be the best mother or father you can be.

2   The impact of a changed life as you work on your relationship with God and begin to walk with Him speaks louder to your child than your failures.

RESOURCE READING

Genesis 44

BECAUSE I SAID SO

*Children, obey your parents in
everything, for this pleases the Lord.*
Colossians 3:20

A child doesn't want to eat the vegetables
on his plate, and though he has asked the
question a million—maybe two million
times—he asks it anyway. He knows it is always
good for a few more seconds of stalling: "Why do I
have to eat my vegetables?"

The parent, however, has just seen the needle
on his patience meter hit the top—the red part
which indicates a very explosive situation. In this
danger zone, parents are liable to all kinds of
unbecoming thoughts and acts. They are prone to
use words which should not be used in front of
children.

Who knows what might happen? But then, the
parent, remembering all the good books about
parenting—about keeping one's temper and
providing a role model for one's child—bites his lip

until it almost bleeds, clenches his teeth and says, "BECAUSE I SAID SO!" Those words are always spoken in capital letters followed by an exclamation point still smoking when it sizzles across the teeth.

That line has been used for centuries. It is what you always say when you have exhausted your patience and you no longer trust yourself not to become violent. So you, having heard those words when you were a child, say that same line to your own child: "BECAUSE I SAID SO!" Hearing those words, a child realizes that he has lost the battle, that

> *Parenting is the raising of children by parents, not the raising of parents by children.*

dialogue has irretrievably broken down, and he had better cultivate a taste for vegetables—fast. Discussion closed.

A slightly more modern version was the wording on a sweatshirt worn by a young mother who was pushing a double-seated baby stroller, one of those affairs that will hold two children plus a couple duffel bags of diapers and bottles. The slogan read, "Because I'm the Mommy—That's Why!"

Now, frankly, as a grandfather who is presently enjoying watching an eighteen-month-old assert his independence just as his mother did some thirty years ago, I understand this whole issue. At some point—preferably very early in the parenting process—parents must learn an important lesson:

Parenting is the raising of children by parents, not the raising of parents by children.

Somebody is going to be in charge, and it had better be Mommy and Daddy, as God so ordered, or else for the next eighteen years, you are in for a very rough ride.

Raising your voice to glass-breaking level and saying, "BECAUSE I SAID SO!" is overkill. Establishing parental authority is not a matter of noise or decibels, but it does involve saying what you mean and meaning what you say. This can be done lovingly and quietly. It shouldn't have to be very often said or done, but the message should come through: "I'm the parent and that settles it." And why should you accept what I've just said? "BECAUSE I SAID SO—THAT'S WHY!"

> INSIGHT
>
> *Leadership—the quiet kind which God wants you to exert in your family—is not a matter of being a bully, a dictator or a boss. It is simply taking control and doing the right thing.*

THINK ON THIS

1 Providing an alternative or choice of two things (both of which are acceptable

to you) may help involve your child in decision-making.

2   When you speak kindly but firmly it saves having to raise your voice several decibels before your child knows that you really mean business.

3   Ask your child to stop what he is doing and look at you before you instruct him. This focuses his attention and eliminates the possibility that you are not being heard.

RESOURCE READING

Colossians 3

RAISING POSITIVE KIDS IN A NEGATIVE WORLD

*The LORD called Samuel a third time, and
Samuel got up and went to Eli and said,
'Here I am; you called me.' Then Eli
realized that the LORD was calling the boy.*

1 Samuel 3:8

In his book *Raising Positive Kids in a Negative World*, Zig Ziglar says that the key to successful parenting isn't what parents do, but what they are.[11] Ziglar is right. "The kid's a chip off the old block," we sometimes say of a youngster who resembles his dad. Or we say, "Like father, like son." Raising positive kids in a negative world begins in your heart, not your vocal chords. It's what you are, not what you say, that counts the most. It's your example that most influences your children.

Anyone who has run a long race always looks back and reflects on the path he just took. He remembers the rough spots; the challenges that could have caused failure. Parents do the same thing, and it doesn't just happen when you walk your daughter down the aisle. It's for a lifetime.

In my file are more letters than I can count from parents who look back and ask, "Where did I go wrong?" In many cases it was not the parent who went wrong. It was the youth who chose to walk a different path.

Compiling the selections for this book has given me a new focus on parenting, both as a dad and grandfather, and as a friend and counselor.

I often see two sets of parents raising their children in the same basic environment and culture. One set of kids go straight and make their parents proud, yet the other kids get derailed, often mortgaging their futures and blighting their hope of getting anywhere in life. Why did this happen?

One powerful factor in raising positive kids is how parents help their children to think for themselves. This gives their kids enough strength to stand alone when they need to.

One powerful factor is how parents help their children think for themselves. This gives their kids enough strength to stand alone when they need to, or walk away from bad situations and withstand negative peer pressures.

Three ingredients help produce positive kids in a negative world.

1 Self-esteem
The first factor is self-esteem, or the child's understanding of who he is in relation to his

parents, his family, and God. This involves handling failures, knowing how to be independent, and having the proper tension between living relevant lives and the pressures of conformity.

2 Self-assurance

The world is no friend to your children. It's tough out there. It's not only the neighborhood bully who is the enemy. Your child may also fight racial prejudice, poor education and training, and a host of other obstacles. He needs faith in God and in himself.

> INSIGHT
>
> *Attitudes are contagious! When you know that your youngster can do something and you convey your quiet confidence in him, that helps him to step out and eventually succeed.*

3 Motivation

Proverbs 22:6 talks of the path that a child should go. You as the parent must help him get started on the right path and provide motivation to choose wisely. This is also where God's will comes into the picture. You must grasp that truth and help guide your youngster morally and spiritually.

Raising positive, godly kids in a negative, ungodly world is one of the greatest accomplishments of life. Your task and your accomplishment are far greater than the world knows. But God knows, and you will have His help as you do your part.[12]

THINK ON THIS

1 Be discerning in what you ask of a child. Obviously, a four-year-old can't hit a ball like an eight-year-old because there is a physical limitation.

2 Understand that girls are better at verbal tasks, boys at physical tasks. Girls also mature faster than boys do. That's how God made them. Don't try to put them into the same mold. Know what your child is capable of doing. Make sure you give him praise and encouragement, not censure and ridicule over failure.

RESOURCE READING

Psalm 37:1-7

RAISING A KID SO STRONG HE WON'T NEED YOU

*Only be careful, and watch yourselves closely so
that you do not forget the things your eyes have
seen or let them slip from your heart
as long as you live. Teach them to your children
and to their children after them.*
Deuteronomy 4:9

How do you raise a kid so strong that he won't need you when you aren't there? That should be the goal of every parent, and there aren't many years in which to lay that kind of foundation. I call it giving your child the gift of self-reliance.

Recently, I've asked myself what it takes to produce self-reliance in teens, to help them be strong enough and self-confident enough that they can distance themselves from what they know is wrong. The pressure to go along, to be like everybody else, to push aside what Mom and Dad say—to just "do it"—is very, very powerful. Helping them make the right choices for themselves is the challenge.

I'm convinced that three powerful factors contribute to producing personal strength in the life of a teenager. The absence of these qualities in the lives of so many today explains the number of teenage pregnancies, the rise of gangs, the use of drugs. What are these factors that produce the strength in your teenager to say no with conviction?

Factor 1: Family identity

This may be the most important factor of all. The presence of Dad in the family along with having great times together make for a solid foundation. I believe that since God designed conception in such a way that two persons—a mother and a father—are necessary to bring a child into the world, He intended both to participate in the process of teaching and raising a child.

Values are established inside the family, and kids grow up with them.

Today they are two basic kinds of families, contend Gary and Ann Marie Ezzo, founders of the ministry Growing Kids God's Way: the interdependent family and the independent family. In the interdependent family, the extended family is important. Traditions, family meals, grandparents, family outings, all are important. Values are established inside the family, and kids grow up with them. Kids are expected to be there for meals, to participate in family discussions, to practice the values established by the parents. Loyalty, teamwork and commitment are not optional. They are expected.

In contrast, the independent family finds significance through relationships outside the family.

Values and worth come from peers, not parents. Self-expression is the norm, and individuality is emphasized.

Factor 2: An independence from the culture and the world that surrounds them
Does this mean teens should be recluses, disconnected from the world? No, but they are to build an ego and self-image strong enough that their self-worth is not derived from the culture and the world surrounding them. They are OK, and they know it. They don't have to "go along" to "get along."

Factor 3: A sense of value and self-worth that helps them understand their true importance
Faith in God, and an understanding of the children's true worth in God's sight and in the minds of their parents are positive forces. You can

> ### INSIGHT
>
> *Children are going to derive their sense of value and self-worth from the individuals and culture that surround them: playmates, caregivers, friends, parents and relatives. Lot's daughters were negatively influenced by the city in which they lived and the wicked people who lived there. Putting distance between you and evil is not only prudent but is essential in raising godly kids.*

raise a youngster so strong that he won't need you. Long ago God instructed, "Train a child in the way he should go, and when he is old he will not turn from it" (Proverbs 22:6). And I would add, "And you will be glad you did!"[13]

THINK ON THIS

1 Who was a significant influence in your life as a child? Why and how did this person influence you?
2 Which means more to your children—members of the family (including brothers, sisters and cousins) or outside friends?
3 Of those outside friends, how many of them are from families holding the same values as you?

RESOURCE READING

Genesis 19

RAISING KIDS GOD'S WAY

Sons are a heritage from the LORD,
children a reward from him. Like arrows in
the hands of a warrior are sons
born in one's youth.
Psalm 127:3-4

When you love your children, there are six gifts which you should give them. These gifts cost nothing in terms of money but are very costly in the currency of time, energy and emotion. All of these six are important in successful parenting and raising kids God's way.

Gift 1 is the gift of yourself.
Some parents give everything to their kids but the gift of themselves. Their kids have the latest in clothes, TVs, Nintendo games, DVDs, CDs and Walkmans—all kinds of things, but not Mom or Dad. The gift of yourself is really the gift of love.

Stop long enough for a reality check: How much of yourself do you give to the child you brought into the world?

Gift 2 is the gift of self-esteem.
When a little boy about five years old went out to dinner with his parents, the waiter took his order along with those of the parents. The little boy later commented, "Gee, Dad, he thinks I'm a real person!" Very early in life we learn self-esteem or self-depreciation. Build self-esteem in your child by:

- Avoiding comparisons with other kids
- Telling your youngster how proud you are of him when he does well
- Accepting him just the same in a failure situation as you would in a success
- Being patient and having realistic expectations
- Realizing that every youngster matures at a different rate

Gift 3 is the gift of self-reliance.
Your goal as a parent should be to raise a kid so strong that when you aren't there, he won't need you! "Just say no!" kids are told when their hormones and their peers say, "Just do it!" Your child will have about the same emotional strength as does your family. When you are strong emotionally, you pass that strength on to him.

Everything you do affects the emotional strength of your child.

Gift 4 is the gift of discerning value versus worth.
Offer a four-year-old money or a bright red toy car.
Which will he take? Obviously, the bright toy. But as
he grows older he's got to learn the difference between
immediate gratification and long-term rewards.

Gift 5 is the gift of self-discipline.
Psychologists conducted a test on the relation of
discipline with
maturity. They placed
one marshmallow in
front of a child and
said, "You may have
this now, but if you
wait until we run an
errand and come back,
you may have two."
They discovered that
children who can defer
instant gratification
became stronger and
more productive as
adults. Kids who have
the strength to wait
develop self-discipline that makes a difference in life.

> **INSIGHT**
>
> *All the expensive gifts in the world cannot replace the gift of yourself to your child— your time, your experiences, your care, your thoughts, your touch, your compassion and your love.*

Gift 6 is the gift of faith in God.
This is the gift which you cannot give unless you
possess it yourself. The baton of faith is passed on
from one generation to another when parents live
what they say and practice what they believe.

How many of these gifts have you given your child?[14]

THINK ON THIS

1   Make a list of the last five gifts you have given to your child.
2   Now make a list of the significant times you and your child have had together compared to your child's doing things with his peers. Which is the longer list?

RESOURCE READING

Colossians 3:12-21

Raising G-rated Kids in an X-rated World

The righteous man leads a blameless life; blessed are his children after him.
Proverbs 20:7

Can you raise G-rated kids in an X-rated world? You bet you can, but it isn't easy. It's the challenge of your life. The following are five guidelines which can help you accomplish your goal.

Guideline 1: Set the example.

God made you a Mommy or Daddy, so assume your responsibility. Nothing in the world—not school or even church—can provide a framework for integrity and character to your child as effectively as you. You are the one who can raise a God-rated kid in an X-rated world of moral and spiritual pollution.

If you are an R- or an X-rated parent, don't expect your kids to be G-rated. You set the example; they learn from you.

Guideline 2: Help your child to be his own person.
Help your child throw off the just-be-like-everyone-else mentality so prevalent today. This requires your putting a certain amount of space between your kids and the world, whose values are far from G-rated. This means you help your offspring to understand, "I don't have to be just like everybody else. It's OK to be me and to be different."

Your kids are going to hear and see a lot of junk outside your home, but having a standard at home clearly says to them, "We don't approve of that stuff, and we won't allow it in our home. We love you too much to let you warp your character with junk." Kids will then know the difference.

You have to guard the moral and spiritual nature of your child.

Guideline 3: Build his character through moral feeding.
I can tell you a thousand situations in which your children will not build character. These include watching most movies, TV and listening to a lot of contemporary music. So you have to guard the moral and spiritual nature of your child. This means Sunday school and church, youth activities, going out as a family and just having fun. You'll also need to monitor what comes into your home and what goes into the mind of your kids. This includes not only what you put on the table but the music that goes into the Walkman your child listens to.

Guideline 4: Reinforce character with a positive peer group.

Make it easy for your kids to be with others whose values are the same as yours. And make it difficult for them to be with other kids who are being raised in a permissive environment without convictions. When you fail to make some decisions, by default you lose your influence for good and for God.

Guideline 5: Empower your child with validation.

The most important thing in the life of a youngster isn't really, "What do my peers think of me?" The truth is that parental approval—hearing Dad say, "I'm really proud of you," or Mom say, "Sweetheart, you really handled that situation well. I couldn't have done it better myself"—is the most meaningful validation in your kids' lives.

INSIGHT

If you live in an R-rated world and think your children will live in a G-rated world, you're wrong! It's only a matter of time until they move quickly to your level, and—be sure of this—once they become teens they will go lower than your level. They won't stop where you draw the line.

You can raise G-rated kids in an X-rated world with God's help and a lot of dogged persistence. It's worth it. It will count and make a difference in tomorrow's world.

Think on This

1 Make sure you know what tapes or CDs your youngsters are listening to. Take time to analyze the lyrics of the songs.

2 Make sure you know something about the movies your kids watch when you are not with them.

3 Protect your kids' minds from the evils that seduce them through the media.

4 If you deny your youngster something— "That's not good for you"—replace it with something positive, something better. It's worth the cost. It's an investment in character and integrity.

Resource Reading

Proverbs 10:1-9

CULT INSURANCE

There is a way that seems right to a
man, but in the end it leads to death.
Proverbs 16:25

ear Dr. Sala," writes a friend, "what can I
do to ensure that my kids will never
become involved in a cult group?" There
are some very positive things that you as a parent
can do to ensure that your children will follow the
Lord and won't get entangled in a cult group.

1 Help your child or teen to develop a warm,
   personal relationship with Jesus Christ.
I believe that it is here where many parents fail,
and the incipient seeds of failure burst forth in
vulnerability. It is one thing to know about Christ;
it is totally another to have a personal relationship
with Him and to know how to sustain that
relationship through prayer, the Word of God, and
fellowship with others in a peer group.

In Greek are two words which are usually translated "knowledge." The first word, *gnosis*, often implies head or theoretical knowledge. The second word, *epignosis*, is a compound of a preposition and the original word which means full or complete knowledge. To have the knowledge of Christ in your head is one thing; to have it in your heart is another. A lot of

> *To have the knowledge of Christ in your head is one thing; to have it in your heart is another.*

youngsters today have confused churchianity with Christianity—the former means a social relationship; the latter a vital, personal relationship.

2 Help your child to know how to defend and substantiate what he or she believes.

To ensure that your youngster doesn't become involved in a cult group, give him a standard of biblical truth by which he can evaluate any group or teaching. Scores of people have become involved in cult groups thinking they were really studying the Bible and following the Lord. They simply didn't know the difference.

A person has to know what a meter is before he can determine if a three-foot yardstick falls short. When it comes to spiritual truths, I've come to the conclusion that very, very few churches are able to do much in laying a firm foundation in the lives of young people.

3 Know what your teenagers are thinking.

Remember, this could be different from what they are saying! Sandy Larsen, who with her husband has a ministry counseling with young people involved in cults, contends that church-related young people are often programmed in such a manner that they come up with the right answers—answers that they really question deep in their hearts. But parents, Sunday school teachers or youth workers feel challenged by their questions, and subsequently kids avoid their reactions by saying the right things—but not really believing them.

> **INSIGHT**
>
> *Generally, the attraction of a cult comes through the affirmation, acceptance and strength of a group, which is often lacking in a family, especially a dysfunctional family. Your personal family can be strengthened by bonds with the church family.*

How do you find out what your teens are thinking? Mostly by listening to them. A few penetrating questions will often prime the pump. Keep in mind, though, that if you come down like a ton of bricks on your teenager every time he says something that isn't quite right on target, there isn't much hope of ever knowing what he is really thinking.

4 Provide the warm supportive environment in your home that cancels out the psychological appeal and support of a cult group.

I admit that some parents have close-knit, warm relationships with their kids but their children still become involved in cult groups. Yet the fact remains that many, if not most, of the young people involved in cult groups are from broken homes or homes where there is little family cohesiveness. Unfortunately the cult group becomes the family the youngster never had.

THINK ON THIS

1   If you have teens or preteens who are dissatisfied with your church (even though your family has been there for years), better check out other churches. Having kids involved in church in their teen years is important.

2   When your youngster is invited to join a youth conference, make sure you know who is sponsoring it, what they believe and who is in charge. You could be exposing your youngster to grave danger.

3   Remember, knowing what you believe is
     prerequisite to teaching your children
     what to believe.

4   Not all religions lead to God. Jesus said,
     "I am the way and the truth and the life.
     No one comes to the Father except
     through Me" (John 14:6).

RESOURCE READING

Galatians 5-6

DRAWING THE LINE

*Cast your bread upon the waters, for
after many days you will find it again.*
Ecclesiastes 11:1

Wise is the parent who draws the line and
says, "The line is not negotiable, and I
will not give in to your yelling and
screaming." We parents are human. We like to
make our kids happy, and we certainly don't relish
arguments with them. But in a culture where
almost anything goes, a loving, thoughtful parent
has to draw the line.

But no matter where you draw the line, your
youngster will push for a bit more. "Everybody else
is doing it!" he'll argue. That's human nature. Go
to the largest cattle ranch in the world and cross
miles of prairie and sagebrush, and there you will
find a cow with its head stuck through the barbed-
wire fence trying to nibble on the grass just beyond
its reach. That's like human nature as well.

A father, concerned, that his four youngsters would get hurt playing in the street in front of their house, drew a chalk line on the pavement and said, "OK, you can play in the street, but stay on this side of the chalk line." When he came home that night—you guessed it—he found his four kids standing on the chalk line.

Many parents didn't draw lines when their kids were young. These children are now paying the price. They are having problems now because they were not trained in the basics by their parents, such as showing up at work on time, driving without drinking and living within the law.

Drawing the line and lovingly enforcing it helps prepare a kid for life.

The fact is that life draws lines that are hard and non-negotiable. When you ignore boundaries, you suffer the consequences. Failing to draw the line is like playing a game with no rules. Sooner or later, there are consequences—severe ones.

Drawing the line and lovingly enforcing it helps prepare a kid for life. It also makes it easier for him as he grows up. How? It takes his peers' pressure off him. He can grouch and say, "I can't do that! My mom won't let me," making you the bad guy, but he doesn't end up in a situation he would prefer to avoid but doesn't know how to.

Setting limitations brings peace to your home. There's an eleven o'clock curfew on Friday and

Saturday nights, and unless something important comes up, that's the way it is, thus preventing arguments.

Drawing the line and staying within the boundaries also teaches a spiritual lesson. God draws the line too, and though there is forgiveness with Him, we still reap the consequences of our failures when we ignore His boundaries.

Galatians 6:7 says, "Don't be misled; remember that you can't ignore God and get away with it: a man will always reap just the kind of crop he sows!" (*TLB*).

Knowing what the boundaries are— whether they are yours or God's—brings security. You know when you are within the framework of acceptable behavior and when you have gone beyond the pale of safety.

INSIGHT

Boundaries provide security from without and within. Knowing that you are within the boundary takes the pressure off and provides peace of mind for you as parent, and for your child.

Wise is the parent who loves enough, cares enough and is strong enough to say, "I love you too much to let you do just anything you want. This is as far as you can go."

Eventually your son or daughter will grow up and say, "Thanks, Mom, thanks, Dad. I'm glad you cared enough to draw the line."

THINK ON THIS

1   Some boundaries are non-negotiable.
    They are fixed and not subject to
    discussion. Some, however, can be
    arrived at together with your child.
2   A youngster should have the right to
    express himself—to disagree without
    being disagreeable—but he needs to be
    willing to accept the decision of a parent.
3   Listening is important. If your child
    knows that he has been heard, he will be
    more willing to accept the boundaries you
    lay down than if he feels that his feelings
    and thoughts weren't considered.

RESOURCE READING

Genesis 27

TRIUMPH OF TOUGH LOVE

*How great is the love the Father has lavished on us, that
we should be called children of God! And that is what we
are! The reason the world does not know us is that it did
not know him. Dear friends, now we are the children of
God, and what we will be has not yet been made known.
But we know that when he appears, we shall be like him,
for we shall see him as he is.*
1 John 3:1-2

Have you as a parent ever felt like giving up
on your teenager who turned his back on
you and God? Then this selection is just
for you. I've called this the "Triumph of Tough
Love." Now here's the question that launches our
discussion: Is it possible for you as parent to
separate your youngster's behavior from your
acceptance of him?

Not only is it possible, it is absolutely necessary.
Sooner or later almost every parent has to say,
"Look, child, I love you, but what you are doing
isn't right and I won't allow it." You reject the
behavior, not the person.

This is the opposite of what one father did. When
his son started smoking pot, the father, who had raised
his three boys on rigid discipline, said, "You either get
rid of that stuff or you get out of the house."

Ultimatums are dangerous. When you say, "You do this, or else..." you are drawing a line and saying, "I dare you to step over it." An ultimatum to a teen or a young adult who considers himself to be mature (when in reality he isn't) is like waving a red flag in front of a bull. In defiance he rears back and says, "Oh yeah—just try me."

You've probably guessed what happened. The youngster left home. With no place to go, he started sleeping in the backseats of parked automobiles until the police found him. It was either go to jail or get off the street. With no place to go and no money, he went back to the pusher and started selling marijuana. In a short while, he graduated to heroin, and by the time the father realized what a tragic mistake he had made, the teenager had become addicted.

To get even with our children for hurting our family pride, we step on them when they need our help the most.

There are times when the situation requires of you the loving action to say, "This is it. You need help and I'm going to see that you get it." That's tough love. However, before you say, "You do this or else," think and pray about the implications and see if there is a better way to handle the situation.

Unconditional love, the tough kind God has for us, and the kind we must have for each other in the family, means acceptance, but it also distinguishes between acceptance and approval. Another thing about unconditional love is that it forgives and leads to self-acceptance and assurance. It's a package.

Paul wrote, "Be ye kind one to another, tenderhearted, forgiving one another, even as God for Christ's sake hath forgiven you" (Ephesians 4:32, *KJV*). The model of God's tough love that encompasses forgiveness is the Father's love for us. Forgiveness isn't something freely extended as the result of the kindness of your heart.

> **INSIGHT**
>
> *Looking beyond the distressing situation to the future helps you see the larger picture. The immediate crisis will pass, but what you do now may determine whether or not you will be part of the future of your teenager. Don't burn your bridges.*

You don't deserve God's forgiveness any more than your child deserves to be forgiven when he has done something terribly wrong. Sometimes we parents do what no animal would ever do: We hit out at our own flesh and blood—our kids who have been taken captive by the lusts of the world. Often we do so because our pride has been hurt, our reputation in the neighborhood has been tarnished, we've been embarrassed by the things our kids have done. To get even, we become hard on them when they need our help the most.

To love without having the love returned demands the unconditional love which God has for us. Paul spoke of it, saying, "God demonstrates his own love for us in this: While we were still sinners, Christ died for us" (Romans 5:8). As Charles Wesley put it, "Died He for me, who caused His pain, for me, who Him, to death pursued? Amazing love! How can it be that Thou, my God, shouldst die for me?"

THINK ON THIS

1   You've got to decide where to draw the line. But remember, once you draw the line and pronounce the ultimatum, "You do this or else!" you had better be willing to live with the "or else!" because that's probably what is going to happen.

2   Before you pronounce an ultimatum, do three things:
    • Make the situation a sustained matter of prayer.
    • Talk over the situation with a friend and make sure you and your spouse are together in what you decide, and;
    • Be ready to live with the consequences of your decision.

RESOURCE READING

1 Corinthians 13 (I suggest that you read this passage every day this week. It's life-changing!)

BEAT THEM
NOW AND THEN TO
KEEP THEM IN LINE?

*Do not withhold discipline from a
child; if you punish him with the rod,
he will not die.*
Proverbs 23:13

When I was a guest professor at Donetsk
Christian University in the Ukraine, I
taught a Family Living class for college
students who had come from all over the former
USSR. When I asked them to write a family
history, many students told about being beaten or
severely punished as children. One young man told
me that when he was growing up in Moscow, it
was acceptable for parents to beat their children
periodically. He said his parents actually believed
that whether or not a child had misbehaved, the
occasional thrashing of a child was good for him.

Does the Bible differentiate between discipline
and punishment? Yes, clearly it does. The word
paideias, usually translated "to discipline" in the New
Testament, is much different from the word *mastigoi*,
which means "to strike, hit or wound." *Mastigoi* was

used of Jesus Christ when He was scourged by the Roman soldiers. *Paideias,* which was also translated "to instruct, train, correct or give guidance to," was used of a father's guidance of his son, or even an instructor's correction of a student.

When a child misbehaves, should he be punished or disciplined? Not wanting to split hairs over meanings, I must point out that there is a vast difference between the two. When a person commits a crime, people are incensed; they cry for justice. They are not so much concerned about what this person does in the future as they are in his paying the price of his wrongdoing. This is punishment.

> *The whole concept of biblical discipline is to teach that what a child has done is wrong and unacceptable.*

But the issue of a child's needing correction is totally different. The focus is not what was done, which was wrong, but what is not going to be allowed. The emotion generating punishment is anger, while the emotion generating discipline is love.

The whole concept of biblical discipline is to teach that what a child has done is wrong and unacceptable. Some parents, not knowing the difference, do punish their children. Far wiser is the parent who knows the difference and learns that discipline is both necessary and effective.

Discipline motivated by love is a winner. Discipline begins with parents who are in control and who convey the importance of that same quality to their kids. The Bible is clear that God disciplines those whom He loves,

bringing them back to the path from which they have strayed. The godly parent who loves his child and disciplines him in love is modeling this great truth.

THINK ON THIS

There are many ways you can provide discipline aside from physical discipline. Make a list. Which of these is most effective? Should you use it in every situation?

RESOURCE READING

Proverbs 23

WHEN YOUR CHILD
NEEDS DISCIPLINE

No discipline seems pleasant at the time,
but painful. Later on, however, it produces
a harvest of righteousness and peace for
those who have been trained by it.
Hebrews 12:11

Divide and conquer is not only the modus operandi of warfare, but it is also the strategy of kids who know that if they can pit parents against each other, they have won the battle. Our English word "discipline" comes from the Latin word *discere*, which means "to know" or in the broader sense, "to discern."

Yet the fact remains that providing discipline for children is one of the most difficult areas of parenting. Regardless of how tired or stressed-out a parent may be, enforcing the teaching-learning process is one of the most important contributions a parent makes to the future of his children.

When a youngster's behavior deteriorates to the point where discipline is necessary, you need to ask some important questions.

"Why has discipline become an issue?"
Kids have an amazing radar system. When you are under stress, kids automatically pick up on that without understanding the pressure you are under. They just sense that Mom or Dad is edgy. Quite often their behavior is an attempt to get your attention.

A child's improper behavior may be his way of saying "You need to spend more time with me!" Or, "I want your attention, and I want it so badly that I am willing to risk getting into trouble to get it."

"Have I made it clear that certain things are totally off-limits in our family, and that when those things are chosen, discipline is the result?"
A parent who takes out his anger on his child treats the youngster unfairly. But the parent who lets children know that some things aren't going to be allowed does his youngster a great favor. He is equipping the youngster for life—which is a far sterner taskmaster than the

Life is a far sterner taskmaster than the parent who loves his child and insists that the youngster learns to do right!

parent who loves his child and insists that the youngster learns to do right!

When behavior becomes a problem, you need to go one step further by asking—

"Am I consistent in what I expect?"

Let's say bedtime is nine o'clock. But you aren't consistent about enforcing it. And then when you are crabby, you yell at your kids because it is after ten and they still aren't in bed. You are sending conflicting messages that create insecurity.

> **INSIGHT**
>
> *Being sensitive to the cause of a problem is a key to helping you deal with it wisely. For example, when a child is really tired, he's apt to fuss and annoy you. "You sit still and be quiet or I'm going to whip you!" Wrong. He doesn't need discipline; he needs sleep.*

One little fellow knew that his dad meant what he said and said what he meant. After the little boy went to bed, he called out, "Daddy, can I have a drink of water?" His father, who knew he was stalling, answered, "No, son, go to sleep." Five minutes later came another plea, "Please, Daddy, can I have a drink of water?" "No, son, and if you ask one more time, I'm going to spank you." For five minutes there was absolute silence, and then a resigned little voice says, "Daddy, when you get up to spank me, can I have a glass of water?"

"What is the best way to deal with a situation that demands discipline?"
How you do it has so much to do with its effectiveness. Anger creates anger, but discipline administered with love produces well-adjusted children who know the difference between right and wrong and choose to do right.

Hebrews 12:11 says, "No discipline seems pleasant at the time, but painful. Later on, however, it produces a harvest of righteousness and peace for those who have been trained by it." So be it.

THINK ON THIS

1   Disciplining a child for what he cannot help (say, a three-year-old who still wets the bed at night) produces anger and frustration. But willful disobedience and defiance are two situations that cannot be ignored. How do you know the difference?

2   Make sure that you have clarified to your child what is right or wrong—what is acceptable or unacceptable—before you discipline.

3   Take a Bible concordance and look up the word "discipline." Jot down each reference. Then read the verses, making notes of the benefits of correction.

RESOURCE READING

Hebrews 12:1-12

BENEFITS OF DISCIPLINE

*A wise son brings joy to his father, but
a foolish son grief to his mother.*
Proverbs 10:1

Motivational speaker and storyteller Ethel Barrett tells of an incident she saw while waiting her turn in a beauty shop. A little boy, about four years of age, started yelling and screaming at the top of his lungs. Most folks tried to ignore the unruly child, but then a gray-haired lady gruffly barked, "Sit down!" The kid, ready to do battle, threw a magazine at her.

Like a drill sergeant, she gave the order again, "Sit down!" and this time she picked him up and sat him in a chair. The little boy let out a blood-curdling scream that was heard miles away. Picking up the magazine, she began to turn the pages and point to the pictures, asking, "What's that?" The little boy still paid no attention and continued to yell. The grandmother kept turning the pages until the little boy had begun responding, naming the things in the pictures.

Finally, the grandmother wiped away the little boy's tears, and he was quite happy when it was her turn to have her hair done. As she prepared to get up she said, "Now you sit here and look at this magazine."

When Ethel Barrett passed by she said, "My, you have an intelligent child with you!"

Discipline enforces the teaching-learning process.

"With me?" said the grandmother.

"I never saw that kid before. I saw he needed discipline and decided to give it to him!"

What does discipline accomplish in the life of a youngster? Here are five things which may well be an encouragement to you, whether you are a parent, a grandparent, an aunt, or a friend.

1 Discipline produces happy, well-adjusted children. Ethel Barrett's story illustrates that point. Discipline isn't pleasant for those who give it and certainly for those who receive it. But discipline produces maturity in life as well as in our relationship with God.

2 Discipline produces security for the child because he knows the boundaries of acceptable behavior. No matter where you set limits, kids will push for just a bit more. However, when children understand how far they can go, there comes a security they can never have when parents won't say, "This is the limit!"

3 Discipline teaches obedience to parental authority.
Discipline gives the knowledge of right and wrong with the motivation to do right. Discipline enforces the teaching-learning process.

4 Discipline helps a child learn to assume responsibility.

Show me a man who is successful, and I'll show you someone who learned personal discipline, whether at home, in school or in the military. One of the traits of successful people is the ability to discipline themselves and subsequently accomplish a given task.

> INSIGHT
>
> *A study of successful people show that at some point in their lives they had to learn how to discipline themselves to be successful.*

5 Discipline provides guidance and security to a child until he or she is old enough to make value decisions on his own.
Discipline means everybody wins—parents and kids alike.

THINK ON THIS

If you grew up in an environment without discipline, your first step is to begin taking small steps of discipline in your own life—promptness, keeping your word, maintaining order. Then study what the Bible says about this whole area of our Christian experience—which is neglected in the preaching and teaching of many churches.

RESOURCE READING

Deuteronomy 11

WHEN PARENTS FAIL TO DISCIPLINE

*He who spares the rod hates his
son, but he who loves him is careful
to discipline him.*
Proverbs 13:24

When Michael Fay, an American teenager
was found guilty of vandalizing a car in
Singapore, he was sentenced to
punishment by caning. Michael Fay drew a
considerable amount of publicity all over the world.
A great deal of public opinion came down on the
side of the courts. "He got exactly what he deserved,"
said many. Some lawmakers were so impressed with
the results that they introduced legislation enabling
authorities to paddle wayward youths. This, they
thought, would be an appropriate way of responding
to juvenile crime and violence.

Others, of course, disagreed with the manner in
which Singapore authorities dealt with juvenile
crime and vandalism. They felt that the boy didn't
deserve the humiliation of having his backside

thumped four times with a cane. They contended that the punishment was too severe, too barbaric, too humiliating.

There is one thing for sure: In Singapore you will not find graffiti defacing buildings and highways. You won't find gum on the sidewalk or trash littering the highways. Laws are rigidly enforced in Singapore and the people know that if you ignore the law, there is a price to pay.

In our desire to be loving, caring, and understanding parents, we have grown soft on discipline. We have done our children a tremendous injustice by allowing them to get away with everything short of murder.

When we cannot discipline ourselves, life has a way of providing that discipline. Take, for example, the sad story of a young woman, a mother of a beautiful little girl now starting school, who will never live to see

> *When we cannot discipline ourselves, life has a way of providing that discipline.*

her daughter graduate from high school. Why? One time she couldn't say no to a friend, and she contracted AIDS. What a price to pay!

I'm also thinking of a gifted and articulate career woman, happily married and wanting a baby of her own. But the sad reality is that she will never cradle her own child in her arms. Her husband of some twenty years brought into the marriage an infection which was eventually cured but left her unable to bear children. What a price to pay, what a terrible thing to inflict on someone you love because you can't discipline yourself and say no to a few moments of pleasure.

> **INSIGHT**
>
> *Learning to discipline ourselves is much like having a burglar alarm in your home but not bothering to turn it on. When you least think that you need it may be the one time when you absolutely need it.*

The Bible says, "Do not be deceived: God cannot be mocked. A man reaps what he sows. The one who sows to please his sinful nature, from that nature will reap destruction; the one who sows to please the Spirit, from the Spirit will reap eternal life" (Galatians 6:7-8). Paul's words are not harsh or opinionated. They simply describe the reality of life.

When we parents fail to discipline ourselves and our children, life ultimately does it for us, and the consequences are cruel and much harsher than that which a Singaporean court decrees.

THINK ON THIS

Make a list of areas in your own life which need improvement. Put the list in your wallet or purse, and get it out every day this week and reflect on it.

RESOURCE READING

Galatians 6:1-10

GOD INSTRUCTS, TEACHES, AND GUIDES

I will instruct you and teach you in the way you should go; I will guide you with My eye.
Psalm 32:8, NKJV

When an acquaintance told me about having to drive across 5,000 kilometers of snow and ice to visit outstations in the frozen wastelands of Siberia, I asked, "How do you know where you are going?"

He replied, "Just a compass!"

"Have you ever heard of a GPS unit?" I inquired.

"A what?" he said.

"It's global positioning by satellite," I explained, telling him that the small handheld unit takes a fix on some fourteen satellites and then pinpoints your location with precise accuracy. His eyes widened with excitement.

That day, I sent an e-mail to our *Guidelines* office. The staff found a GPS unit, sent it by overnight express to a friend who the next day flew some 7,000 miles and brought it with him. Within three days, the man who would have used his compass had a far more accurate means of knowing where he was as he started his journey across Siberia in winter.

Direction in our world is important; in your personal life, it is even more. Many explorers have died of thirst or hunger, knowing that water or food was nearby but unable to find it.

In Psalm 32:8 (*NKJV*), God gave a promise to David. Three verbs provide guidance when it comes to knowing where to go with your life. God said, "I will instruct you and teach you in the way you should go; I will guide you with My eye". How does He provide direction? First, He says, "I will instruct you." Second, "I will teach you." Third, "I will guide you with My eye."

As a loving Father, God instructs us, teaches us and guides us with His eye.

Teaching and instruction are entirely different. You can read a book on computer science and be completely lost. Better to take a class where a teacher gives instructions. Better still for someone to sit down with you and say, "Look, I'll show you how to do it. You start by turning on the computer…" Having someone show you step-by-step is a lot easier and more meaningful than reading a book or even taking a class.

When God says, "I will guide you with My eye," does it mean just what it says? Can you communicate with a simple look?

My son Steve would say that you can! When he was seven, one Sunday evening he positioned himself on the front row of the church where I was pastoring and proceeded to launch spit wads in a variety of directions. His mother, who was playing the piano, was no threat. When I caught him glancing furtively at me, I narrowed my eyes to communicate this message: "Stop it. Now!"

Thinking that I would forget about it later, he ignored me. It was time for me to speak, so I stood and addressed the group saying, "Before our study tonight, we will have one more song." As the song leader grabbed a book and searched for something to sing, I went down from the platform, took my son by the hand and led him down the side aisle to the patio, where we had a heart-to-heart talk.

> **INSIGHT**
>
> *Just as we can give direction to a child by simply catching his eye, so God by His Spirit will give us guidance when we are sensitive to Him.*

The singing was just finishing when the two of us came down the aisle. Steve was muffling furtive sobs as I preached. People have long since forgotten what I spoke on, but those who were there will never forget what I did.

As a loving Father, God instructs us, teaches us and guides us with His eye. How can we miss His will and purpose for our lives? Yes, He still guides with His eye! May we understand clearly what He is saying lest we face the consequences of disobedience.

THINK ON THIS

Is your relationship with your youngster close enough so that you can communicate simply by looking at each other? Do you find that one child is more sensitive to you than another?

RESOURCE READING

Psalm 32

TALKING TO YOUR KIDS ABOUT SEX

*So God created man in his own image, in the
image of God he created him; male and
female he created them.*
Genesis 1: 27

These days, sex is being talked about almost anywhere—on TV, in the movies, on talk shows on radio, and in casual conversations. Almost everybody is talking about sex, that is, except parents.

Take your youngster to the beach. Take him to the grocery store, and in the checkout line your child could see lurid covers of some tabloids and magazines.

The problem is, however, that much of what a child sees in the ads is not how God intended sex should be in our lives.

Why talk to your children about sex? Because your failure to deal with this important topic means that he may get a mixed-up or perverted picture of the whole thing.

Why are we adults so hesitant to deal with this subject in a factual, straightforward manner—putting it in the light that God intends, helping our kids to understand why we must respect one another and be aware that our bodies are private? Perhaps the answer is that we grew up with hang-ups because our own parents were too embarrassed when we asked questions, leaving us with the distinct feeling that sex is something that should not be discussed.

The following guidelines will help you know how and when to talk to your kids about this important topic.

Realize that your failure to deal with the subject will only push your child to get sex education from another source.
The source could be another child, a pornographic magazine, a web site or some distorted and perhaps perverted source. Sex is part of life and should neither be avoided nor considered embarrassing. Sex education is too personal, too important to be left to school or church. It's a parent's responsibility. Period.

> *Sex education is too personal, too important to be left to school or church. It's a parent's responsibility.*

You need to get the facts straight yourself.
I am amazed at the ignorance of many adults when it comes to the functions of the human body and how a baby is conceived. Procreation is one of the absolutely amazing phenomena of existence. When you talk to a little child about sex, avoid vulgar or slang terms. Children can understand proper terms.

Answer questions as they arise.
A rule of thumb is to tell a child what he wants to know. Give him an answer that satisfies, and do it when the question is asked.

Put into practice in your home the values that you feel are important.
In a real sense you are the sex-education program your youngster needs. This includes hugs and goodnight kisses and the fact that Mom and Dad love each other, and that we respect each other's privacy. If you have a good marriage, your kids will see that. But your children and teens need to understand that sex is not for kids but for married adults. By teaching your child that sex is a beautiful, meaningful relationship for a husband and wife, you are helping him or her understand a value which has been neglected and badly distorted.

INSIGHT

Your child is going to get sex education. The only question is from what source. Either the sources mentioned here or from you—it's your call.

Make sure your child understands that his or her body is private.
We can't ignore the danger that confronts kids growing up today: Strangers cannot be trusted. An attitude of suspicion or distrust of everyone isn't necessary, but keeping the kind of a relationship with

your youngster that makes it easy for him or her to talk to you is important.

Think about it, and then talk about it. It's all part of your job as a parent.

THINK ON THIS

Answer questions as they come up, giving enough information to satisfy. Use straightforward language, in a matter-of-fact manner.

RESOURCE READING

Genesis 1

SEX IS NOT FOR KIDS

They made me the keeper of the vineyards;
but my own vineyard have I not kept.
Song of Solomon 1:6, KJV

We're living in a global village, and whether or not we like it, life has become much the same for people in Manila, Los Angeles, Bucharest or Sydney. We can eat at the same fastfood, wear the same brand of clothes and watch the same TV program. All these produce staleness in life and predictable behavior.

In the same week, two shocking articles came across my desk, both dealing with teens, both pointing out that kids between the ages of ten and fourteen are far more sexually active than their parents or teachers have any inkling of. One article, a *Time* magazine feature, "Where'd You Learn That?" described American teens.[15] The other article came from the *Manila Bulletin*, some 8,000 miles removed from the US, and was captioned, "Filipino 10 to 14-year-olds engaging in sex? You'd be surprised!"

Both articles cited several factors in the tremendous increase in sexual activitity among kids hardly old enough to shave or wear perfume. These are: access to media and the sexual exposure it brings, absentee parents or working parents who are uninvolved in the lives of their teens, and peer pressure.

"Three powerful forces have shaped today's child prodigies," says *Time*, "a prosperous information age that increasingly promotes products and entertains audiences by titillation; aggressive public-policy initiates that loudly preach sexual responsibility, further desensitizing kids to the subject; and the decline of two-parent households, which leaves adolescents with little supervision."[16]

You are a parent, and there is nothing under God's heaven which substitutes for your presence.

I have to ask two sobering questions: First, where have the parents gone? Second, why is the church so silent and ineffective in making a difference in our culture and society?

Parents who are not there when a youngster comes home from school by default allow the media to become the major influence in their child's life. Dragging your youngster to church on Sunday or casually asking, "How did your day go?" isn't enough to counter the impact of five hours of television a day.

There is no substitute for being there, for knowing who your child is speaking to on the telephone, or knowing whether your kid is doing homework or watching MTV. There is nothing under God's heaven which substitutes for your presence.

Why can't the church be more than a voice of conscience crying, "Naughty! Naughty! Don't do that!"? In a list of items asking church kids to rate where they need spiritual help, the vast majority of youth said, "The church tells me what *not* to do, but not *what* to do." They have a point.

Sexuality is a part of life, and the Bible has a lot to say about its place in our lives. God didn't give us the advice in Scriptures to take away the fun or excitement but to give us guidance and happiness.

INSIGHT

Our neglecting to talk openly and specifically about sex sends a message of indifference. Talking about it lets our teens know that we care and accept responsibility for what they do. It also gives us the opportunity to talk about how God views this part of our lives.

When the Bible decries premarital sex it is with reason that goes far beyond what we think of as Victorian prudishness. Apart from marriage, sexual relations will never meet the deep emotional needs of either partner. But the emotional scars and damage from casual sex can take a lifetime to heal.

Regardless of what's happening in our culture and society, there is good news: God's purpose in our lives continues to be beneficent and purposeful. It's still the good news in a bad-news world.

THINK ON THIS

1   How many afternoons last week was your teen at home alone?
2   Have you talked about STD, AIDS, and pregnancy with your teen?
3   Is it possible that your teenager may be sexually active but you prefer not to know about it?

RESOURCE READING

Ephesians 6:1–4

LAYING THE FOUNDATION OF FAITH

These commandments that I give you today are to be upon your hearts. Impress them on your children. Talk about them when you sit down at home and when you walk along the road, when you lie down and when you get up.
Deuteronomy 6:6–7

If you are depending on an hour's attendance at local church to offset the influence of the secular world in the life of your child, forget it! You are up against tougher competition than you can handle. Altogether too often we go to a church not too far away from home where we sit for an hour while our children are in Sunday school or Junior church. The kids sing songs, color pictures, and have cookies and juice before they listen to a Bible story or a mini sermon.

But your youngster spends around thirty-five hours in public school, and, along with the 3 Rs, he will get sex education, evolution and social theories which run counter to much of what he learns in church. In addition, there's the impact of the great educator which is prominently displayed in your family or living room, otherwise known as TV set—or should we call it the video worship center?

Figures show that in most households, the TV is on at an average of five-and-a-half hours a day. By the time your youngster graduates from high school, he will have seen 15,000 to 20,000 hours of television and will have witnessed 25,000 acts of violence including rape and murder.

But won't kids just "pick up" Christian values by growing up in a Christian home? Sure, just like they pick up science and math or become excellent musicians by just growing up in a home where parents have those abilities. It is true that some things are caught not taught, but when it comes to offsetting the secular influence that surrounds children, we need a frontal attack.

Why not set aside time each day, even if it is as brief as five minutes following a meal, when you as a family touch God together?

After God gave the Ten Commandments at Mt. Sinai, Moses admonished the people to walk in the ways of the Lord and to teach these commandments to their children. He said:

> "These commandments that I give you today are to be upon your hearts. Impress them on your children. Talk about them when you sit

at home and when you walk along the road,
when you lie down and when you get up."
Deuteronomy 6:6–7

He put the responsibility of morality and integrity on the shoulders of parents, who in turn, convey spiritual truths to their children. You feed your kids daily, right? You expect them to study their lessons daily. You want them to practice daily to achieve a certain level of proficiency in music. Why not set aside some time each day, even if it is as brief as five minutes following a meal, when you as a family touch God together? This prayer time can be tremendously meaningful in the lives of your children.

Most people call this time "Family Devotions" or "Family Worship." No matter

INSIGHT

With our busy lives it becomes very easy to assume that our kids will get the core experience of our faith by just being in a Christian home and by taking part in church-related activities. Don't assume anything. Take time to plant the Word in the heart of a child and you will be amply rewarded when you see it bear fruit in the teenager or young adult he becomes.

what you call it, it's important. Several ingredients should go into the mix:

1   Scripture, including memorizing portions of the great Book which stay with your children forever;
2   Praying for one another's needs and the needs of the world; and
3   Caring about each other as families should.

There are some things which need to be done in time... for eternity!

THINK ON THIS

For family devotions:
1   Use a modern translation of Scripture.
2   Involve all the members of the family.
3   Never allow older children to make fun of what younger children say or pray about.
4   Use variety.
5   Make sure you use the mix of the three ingredients suggested.
6   Reward children when they have excelled in memorization and application.

(Note: Incentives are means of affirming excellence, not bribery to do what a child doesn't really want to do.)

RESOURCE READING

Deuteronomy 6:1–7

A Culture of Violence

*The LORD examines the righteous, but the
wicked and those who love
violence his soul hates.*
Psalm 11:5

Dear Dr. Sala, should I let my three-year-old boy play with toy guns?" asks a mother who listens to *Guidelines*. She says, "Even if I don't buy him toy guns, he takes his finger and points it and says 'Boom! Boom!'" In a culture of violence, how does a mother put a barrier between violence and her child?

No generation of children has ever been raised in a culture that has so tolerated and condoned violence as ours. TV, movies, computer games, and the Internet have wiped out the demarcation between reality and fantasy. Absentee or disinterested parents who are too busy to make a difference in the lives of their children have defaulted on the responsibility of teaching the difference between right and wrong.

On the question of why there is so much violence among the youth today—an issue forced upon us after the massacre at Columbine High School in Littleton, Colorado—the following response from an eighteen-year-old by the name of Sarah Roney was widely circulated on the Internet:

> "We live in a loosely-tied society, a culture dedicated to death. If you don't want the kid, kill it. If you don't want to live out the rest of your God-given days, kill yourself. Or better yet, have someone else come help you do it. I guess no matter how horrible or gruesome or gut-wrenching it may be, it was just a matter of time before someone got that 'killing-as-a-means-to-an-end' idea stuck in their head for the part between birth and death as well. Everything that happens in a family and cities and states and countries is the mirror image of the big picture."

No generation of children has ever been raised in a culture that has so tolerated and condoned violence as ours.

This young woman faults parents for the attitudes and dismal conduct of her generation. Parents who are not there for their kids; parents who (in her words), never say, "If you don't shape up by the time I count to three..." and then really count to three. She adds sadly, "We are running wild and pretty soon we're going to be too far from home to ever get back."

I am not ready to lose any of the next generation. Every casualty is someone's son or daughter, a person of value and worth in the sight of God. Jesus said, "For the Son of Man has come to seek and to save that which was lost" (Luke 19:10, *NKJV*).

THINK ON THIS

INSIGHT

Our sensibilities were shocked when a six-year-old boy found a loaded gun, took it to school and pulled the trigger in a classroom, taking the life of a girl in his class. While the little boy's future will be forever tainted, the little girl was deprived of ever having a future.

1   Do you have firearms in your home? Are they locked? Do they have trigger locks? Are the ammo and the firearm separated?
2   While it is highly unlikely that you can completely keep your children from playing with toy guns (whether they are squirt guns or cap guns), you can minimize violence by not buying toys, computer CDs or video games that encourage violence.
3   Find out what wholesome, educational videos and games which are also entertaining and

positive are available. (Yes, there are plenty of
them on the market. Take the time to check
them out.)

4 Don't hesitate to return to the store any
   game, toy or video that promotes violence.

RESOURCE READING

Ephesians 6

YOU CAN ALWAYS TELL A TEENAGER (BUT YOU CAN'T ALWAYS TELL 'EM VERY MUCH)

Train a child in the way he should go,
and when he is old he will
not turn from it.
Proverbs 22:6

Back in the days when computers booted under DOS, I put a line in my autoexec.bat which puts a message on the screen reading, "Remember, this too shall pass!" That's also the way it is with those years called teen years. When you've got a teenager in the house, you sometimes wonder, *Will we survive until he is on his own?* You've got to remember, "This too shall pass!"

For many today the emotional passage from childhood to adulthood is like surviving a tornado or a hurricane. It's a battle. Passing from childhood to adulthood is an important period in a youngster's life. Psychologist Dr. Henry Brandt says, "Your children will most need your guidance between ages sixteen and twenty." Yet often it is during those years that they are the most difficult for parents to handle.

Lest I leave the wrong impression, especially with my teenage friends, I must clarify that not all teenagers are struggling with drugs, alcohol or their sexuality. On the contrary, thousands and thousands of young men and women are working hard, studying, talking to adults (even parents), attending church, and are involved in community affairs, preparing to take their places in the world of the twenty-first century. A growing number of teenagers are committed to Jesus Christ and to biblical principles. But they are the ones you don't hear about. (Ever seen a sign which reads, "Nice dog, does not bite!"?)

Sadly enough, it is usually the exception which draws the printer's ink and the feature in the evening news. In high school and college campuses today a quiet number of student groups meet under the sponsorship of Inter-Varsity Christian Fellow-ship, Campus Crusade for Christ, Athletes in Action and local Bible study groups. They are providing answers to the questions of youth, helping them traverse the troubled waters of adolescence.

Needed: More models, fewer critics; more prayer, less preaching.

I am convinced that when we see a teenager who has failed, we are often looking at the product of parental failure. A child learns half of everything he needs to know by age three, and three-fourths by age seven. In far too many cases, during those important pre-school years a youngster is deprived of instruction and care and left to grow up with a TV set for a tutor and a baby-sitter for a surrogate mother.

In some cases parents can't help the fact that they have to work. But you can still raise your children positively by being the person God would have you to be. You can achieve this by:

1 Taking your youngster to church—and staying;
2 Turning off the TV set and reading to your child;
3 Teaching your child right from wrong; and
4 Striving to be the person you really want your child to become.

Too often it is not until we are confronted with tragedy that we get serious about what's happening to our teens. Then we parents put the blame on our children's friends, teachers and the culture that surrounds us—when the real problem is us. We need more models, fewer critics; more prayer, less preaching; fewer who tell kids what to do and more who do it. May God help us! And yes, He will.

Think on This

1   When you sense that your teenager wants to talk, you better listen, or the time may come when you would give almost anything to know what's going on in his head.
2   How much unstructured time do you spend with your teens? What do you do together for just plain fun?
3   Asking your teener, "What do you think about...?" helps open topics for discussion.

Resource Reading

Proverbs 19:1-18

UNDERSTANDING
TEENAGERS

*The king was shaken. He went up to
the room over the gateway and wept. As he
wept, he said: "O my son Absalom! My son,
my son Absalom! If only I had died instead
of you—O Absalom, my son, my son!"*
2 Samuel 18:33

For some, those teenage years are more like
a battle to be fought than a transition to be
experienced. But for others, those years are
a very good time when a teenager grows to maturity,
becoming the young adult that a parent hoped he
would be.

Youth has been described as a transition from the
organization of childhood to the disorganization of
youth, resulting in the reorganization of adulthood.

Mark Twain was right when he said, "Life would
be infinitely happier if we could only be born at the
age of eighty and gradually approach eighteen." But
no one chooses at what age he is born. Neither do
you choose your parents. For good or bad, you're
stuck with what you've got.

Being the parent of a teenager requires the
balance of a tightrope walker and the skill of a

diamond cutter. One of the reasons it's tough being the parent of a teenager is that the goals of a parent and a teenager are usually at cross-purposes.

What is the goal of a teenager? Independence. And what is the goal of a parent? Maturity. Independence to a teenager is "freedom to do anything I want!" which can result in irresponsibility. But maturity to a parent is making right decisions, which results in responsibility.

Recently I planted a tree in my front yard—a gangly little tree with three branches. Since the tree isn't strong enough to withstand a strong wind and certainly not a climbing child, I had to put stakes to support the three branches. They are temporary, however. As soon as the tree is strong enough to support itself, those stakes have to come down. And the sooner the better! So is it with our children. Support is necessary, but only until a teenager is able to withstand the winds and pressures of life today— something which a great many teenagers are not doing very well.

Support is necessary, but only until a teenager is able to withstand the winds and pressures of life today.

The psalmist likens children to arrows in the hands of an archer (see Psalm 127:4-5). Anyone who has ever held a bow in his hand and notched an arrow learns quickly that hitting the target has everything to do with how firmly you hold the bow and how you release the arrow.

Pull the bowstring back too far or hold onto it too long and you will overdrive the target. But pull it back only a little way and release it too soon and your arrow will fall short of the target. So it is with teenagers. Hold on to them too long and you have rebellion and anger, but release them too soon and they fall short of the target and get into trouble.

Unfortunately, there is no scale anywhere in the world that says your teenager is ready to handle life at age sixteen or seventeen or at five-foot-seven or at six-three. Every teenager is different. Some are quite mature at fourteen, and others at age nineteen still play with their toy boats in the bath.

> **INSIGHT**
>
> *One of the major reasons that the teen years are different is that the goals of parents and their teens are at cross-purposes. Understanding this gives you a framework for conflict resolution.*

The psalmist wrote, "Sons are a heritage from the LORD, children a reward from Him" (Psalm 127:3). It's true—even of teenagers!

THINK ON THIS

1   While some things are non-negotiable (morality, respect for parents, honesty, etc.), there are some issues which can be negotiated. What are some of those in your family?

2   When you parents do not stand together, what kind of a message does this send to your teen?

3   When you suspect that your mate said no to something your teen wants to do, ask, "Did you talk with your Mom/Dad about this? What did she/he say? Well, that's what I say as well." Remember, you parents either hang together or your children hang you separately.

RESOURCE READING

2 Samuel 18

Ten Commandments for Parents of Teens

*Fathers, do not embitter your children,
or they will become discouraged....
Whatever you do, work at it with all
your heart, as working for the Lord.*
Colossians 3:21, 23

One of the reasons it's difficult being a teenager is that emotional maturity rarely matches physical maturity. It's tough being a teenager, probably more so today than ever before, but it's not hopeless. Parents can support their teenagers by being a coach, a teacher, a chaplain, a mentor, a model and, hopefully, a friend as well. Teen years can either be a blessing or a battle, and the parents—not the teenager—usually decide which it will be.

What can parents do to make their children's transition from childhood to adulthood easier? Plenty! Here are "Ten Commandments for Parents of Teens":

Commandment 1: Thou shalt remember that the teen years are a transitional time.
A teenager is in the process of becoming. Teen years are marked by three things:

1 ambivalence (both a child and an adult
  are battling for the same body);
2 growth; and
3 peer pressure.

Commandment 2: Thou shalt be a parent.

Parenting is the raising of children by parents, not the raising of parents by children. You are in charge!

Commandment 3: Thou shalt keep the channels of communication open.

A child becomes a teenager one day at a time. Communication doesn't stop at age thirteen. If it ceases, it is usually, though not always, because the parents haven't been there to listen. Scores of teens and parents communicate openly and freely, and bring each other into their respective worlds.

Commandment 4: Thou shalt sift the trivial from the important.

Parents need to ask, "Will this do damage, or does it just annoy me?" If you saw a four-year-old playing with a knife, you'd do something fast. Drugs, alcohol and promiscuous sex will do damage too—for life.

Commandment 5: Thou shalt use sarcasm and criticism sparingly.

Teens come up with statements that are real shockers, and they do it in a matter-of-fact sort of way. Strive to help your teenager see cause and effect—like what happens when a 14-year-old girl chooses to have a baby—instead of criticizing everything she does.

Commandment 6: Don't impose your unfulfilled ambitions on your teenager.

Discover what your teen's unique gifts are and guide him accordingly. That's part of what Proverbs 22:6 advises: "Train a child in the way he should go, and when he is old he will not turn from it." Your child might never make it to med school but he might be a computer whiz. Go with the flow of the natural aptitudes and abilities which God gave him.

INSIGHT

Generally you get from your child's teen years what you expect: They can be an ongoing battle or a wonderful time of self-realization.

Commandment 7: Thou shalt differentiate between acceptance and approval.

Sooner or later, almost every parent has to convey this message: "Look, I love you but I don't like what you are doing. I think it is wrong." But separate your teen from his or her problem. Be careful that your teen doesn't feel rejected even if you disapprove of his or her action.

Commandment 8: Thou shalt give your child unconditional love.

Never base love on performance.

Commandment 9: Thou shalt give of your time as well as your resources.

It's a tragedy to give your child money, education and culture while withholding the most important gift of all—yourself.

Commandment 10: Thou shalt surround your child with a fence of prayer.

The time may come when a teenager may ignore your advice and spurn your wisdom, but he cannot escape your prayers.

Think on This

1   Realize that teens communicate within their own time frame—not yours—which means that if you don't listen to them when they want to talk, the time may come when you would give anything to have a meaningful conversation with them but they don't want to.

2   A child becomes a teen one day at a time. If communication is poor between a parent and a teen, it has been that way for a long time.

3   Lay the groundwork for communication by having unstructured time together.

Resource Reading

Ephesians 5:15-6:4

217

Is Anyone Listening?

*Do not be amazed at this, for a time is
coming when all who are in their graves will
hear his voice and come out—those who
have done good will rise to live, and those
who have done evil will rise
to be condemned.*
John 5:28-29

L ooking back, the mother said that the
problems started with her 19-year-old son
when he was not accepted by the school
he wanted to attend. He then started drinking
heavily and smoking pot. "Makes me feel better," he
said. His appearance took a hit too. He had been
pretty clean and well-groomed, but now his hair is
long and dirty. He stopped bathing regularly and was
withdrawn and sullen. He often shut himself in his
room and listened to rock music. "I wish I were
dead," he once told a friend.

When his mother would ask him to come out of
his room and spend time with the family, he would
yell, "Leave me alone—I'm all right!" He gave away
his prized collection of CDs and cassettes—the music
that he listened to hour after hour.

Then it happened. Suddenly and unexplainably, he ended his life with an overdose of drugs. A terse suicide note said, "I'm sorry for having messed up my life, but there is no way out."

When the tragedy struck, people said, "How could he do that? He had everything to live for. Something must have snapped!" But the fact was his death was neither sudden nor without warning.

Almost everything I have described was a warning that no one seemed to notice. Are there signs friends and parents should see that tell us something is wrong, something very serious? Yes, but too often we see them only in retrospect.

Never, under any circumstances, should even the casual threat of suicide be taken lightly.

What are some of those indications that things are not right?

1 Isolation and loneliness
2 Contacts with other people—especially authority figures, close friends and family—become shallow and meaningless
3 A preoccupation with death
4 Changes in sleep and eating patterns; those changes go both ways—from habitual sleep to insomnia, from eating practically nothing to eating so much there are rapid weight gains
5 A loss in interest in what has previously been meaningful—school, music, sports or work

6 A breakdown in communication as the person becomes withdrawn and introspective

7 An uncharacteristic display of generosity—even the tidying up of a room that is usually left like a disaster zone

8 Comments about suicide which may be a far more frank assessment of a situation than anyone realizes at the time

9 Depression and lethargy

Never, under any circumstances, should even the casual threat of suicide be taken lightly. People usually talk about what they eventually do.

What should you do when some of these signs are present? The head of a suicide prevention hotline suggests three things: Listen, listen, listen. He believes that most suicides are a desperate cry for someone to be heard.

Skip the advice. Don't waste your breath saying, "Snap out of it—everything is going to be OK." Save the sermons on how much that person has to live for. Instead listen and take seriously the cry of a depressed

INSIGHT

When a youth takes his life, people say, "How could this have happened? There was nothing that made us aware of his problem." The fact is, however, that he had been giving signals for some time but no one picked up on them.

person whose problem may not seem very big to you but is life-threatening to him.

If what I have described is a picture of someone you know, get help for that person. It is far better to confront now than to regret it forever. For some youth today, life doesn't appear to be terribly hopeful, yet to know that someone cares and will listen helps banish despair and brings hope. Where there is life, there is yet hope.

THINK ON THIS

1   If someone you know ever threatens to take his life, then says, "I didn't mean it!" you must not take that lightly. Remember, people usually talk about what they do.

2   Resist the desire to moralize or pass judgment on what your teen may say before you give the whole situation a full hearing. Then approach a situation with which you disagree, saying, "How do you think God views this situation? How about taking some time to look up some Scriptures together?"

RESOURCE READING

John 10

TEEN SUICIDES

For to me, to live is Christ and to die is gain.
Philippians 1:21

The number of teen suicides has reached alarming proportions today, and this is happening not just in the United States but worldwide. In the US, suicide is the second leading cause of death for teens, and overall the number of teen suicides has increased by 300 percent in the last thirty years. For every youth who takes his life, there are thirty to fifty attempts by others.

In Japan the youth suicide rate has so alarmed civic officials that national programs of education have been established to stop the tragic loss of life.

Suicide is taking the lives of some of our finest, most talented young men and women. These suicides seem to say: "Life has lost its purpose and meaning and I've given up on the hope that it can ever be different."[17] Understanding the reasons why young men and women take their lives may help to prevent this ever happening to your family.

As the result of counseling and working with numerous families who have experienced youth suicides, I can isolate four factors that, I believe, contribute to the desperation of youth—resulting in suicide.

1 Inexperience.
As an adult you have faced challenges and pretty tough situations before, and with God's help, you made it—you got through. As a result, when you face problems that seem insurmountable, you do not quit or give up. You hang on and trust God. But kids have not been through as much trouble and hard times as you have. When they are confronted with loss or tragedy or depression, they feel that there is no way out and often despair of life.

2 The inability of youths to live up to their parents' expectations.
This is especially true in Japan, where the failure to pass high school or college entrance exams means the end of the education road. Often when the kids fail, they feel they have disgraced their families, and the humiliation is too great for them to bear. When parents have set up goals that are too high for the youth, or even the youth sets up for himself goals too high to attain, there is a problem. The inability to cope with that problem is one of the factors which has caused the suicide rate to jump drastically.

3 Pessimism in our world which kids can't handle.

The words of the songs sung by many of today's rock or heavy metal groups focus on dark themes—drugs, death and despair. Listening to those negative messages hour after hour, day after day becomes a burden kids can't bear. Without realizing that there is another side to the dark world, they often lose hope and give up on life.

> **INSIGHT**
>
> *One of the reasons for the pessimism and fatalism in the lives of some teens today is that they have not lived long enough to encounter difficult situations and see God bring them through. Lacking the experience an adult may have, they feel despair and hopelessness.*

4 A lack of faith which offsets despair and despondency.

Sharrel Keyes was a suicide candidate. She tells about her experience in *His* magazine. She says,

"The summer I started graduate school all of the superficiality and meaninglessness converged and pushed me into a crisis. I had to find some answers. Since I had just graduated with a minor in Philosophy and Religion, I turned back to my texts for answers. I read the Existentialists, who said there is no meaning except in the present. There is no ultimate why... There is nothing, simply nothing. I finally saw that the logical conclusion to their position was suicide. If there is no reason to be here, then there is no reason to be here now."[18]

Fortunately two things happened to Sharrel that saved her life. The first was that she discovered C.S. Lewis and found a God who is holding everything together in a plan far bigger that she could see. And then she saw the irrationality of taking her own life through the suicide of a close friend.

Despair is banished by even the slightest faith in God. A faith that looks beyond the circumstances to His ability and willingness to change things. Faith is believing promises about the future with few visible guarantees in the present, but it is this that gives you the assurance that life is meaningful. God lives and will honor the promises of His Word.

THINK ON THIS

Strive to help your kids know that no matter how difficult or hopeless a situation; no matter how desperate, how far from God he may think he is, there is hope because there is God. This truth can take any person through his darkest hour.

RESOURCE READING

1 Samuel 28

YOU CAN'T ALWAYS FIX IT

As for me, far be it from me that I
should sin against the LORD
by failing to pray for you.
1 Samuel 12:23

D ear Dr. Sala," writes the parent of a college freshman, "our son received D's and F's on his report card and will not be allowed to go back to college this Fall. Furthermore, he won't listen to our counsel or advice. What should we do?" The letter which I've just shared is a composite of more than a few which have come to us recently. How much should a parent do? What does a parent really owe his youngster who is no longer a child but acts like one?

I'm convinced that the most challenging and often frustrating years of parenting, at least for some, are not when your kids are small, when you say, "Pick up your toys!" and your youngster responds with minimal persuasion. They are the years between the ages of sixteen and twenty-four, when a young person is convinced that he is fully mature, but the parents know that he is not emotionally mature enough to handle some situations.

When do you give advice? When do you bite your tongue and keep your mouth shut? When do you dip into your meager savings to finance higher education, and when do you say, "It's time for you to go to work and support yourself"? Ready for some simple, clear-cut answers?

I'm sorry to disappoint you, but I don't have any. Simplistic answers don't fit every situation. Here's why. Kids mature at different rates. One youngster

A wise parent strives to help a youngster understand he is responsible for his own life.

may be mature at fifteen. Another may still be a ten-year-old in a nineteen-year-old's body. One kid knows exactly what he wants to do with his life and does it. Another changes his major in college six times before settling down. One youngster makes his bed. Another, with the same parents, has a room which is an absolute disaster zone—off-limits to all but the brave.

A wise parent strives to help the youngster understand that he is responsible for his own life. You love your kids, you feed them, you guide them, but ultimately they are responsible for their own choices.

I have to admit that the young adulthood years for my three children were a most fulfilling time of parenting, a whole lot more fun for us than diapers and dishwater hands. But I can tell you one thing for

INSIGHT

At some point you have to say about your young adult, "Lord, there's nothing else I can do. Will You please take over and do what I cannot do?" then leave the situation in His hands.

sure, when your teenager makes the decision to do right and to walk with the Lord because it is what he wants to do—not what you want done—you'll sleep better at night.

THINK ON THIS

1 Have you taken prayer seriously? To find out more about prayer, work through my book *Touching God: 52 Guidelines for Personal Prayer* available in your local Christian bookstore or at OMF Literature Inc.

2 The Bible tells us to pray about everything, and everything means exactly that—your teenager and his problems, when to talk about issues, when to confront, when to say, "I love you too much to let you do this" or just pray, simply awaiting God's timing about a situation.

RESOURCE READING

Genesis 49

AND YOUR CHILDREN
AFTER YOU

*But as for me and my household, we
will serve the LORD.
Joshua 24:15*

"Dear Dr. Sala," wrote a father well into his
seventies, "one of my greatest heartaches is
that my children are not living for the Lord.
They were all raised in a Christian home. In fact, my
wife and I have spent most of our lives in the Lord's
service, but more than anything else, we would like
to see them come back to Him before we die."

Nothing can be more distressing than feeling
strongly about certain values, including our
relationship with God, and then seeing our children
reject those values and turn their back on God. I have
received scores of letters from you who have
unburdened your heart, laden with guilt, because
you are convinced that you did something wrong. In
many cases, it is because your child has a mind of his
own and has chosen to walk an uncertain path.

Can we as Christian parents hold on to the expectation that God will honor His Word and, in time, draw the hearts of our children toward Him? Are there definite promises to which we can cling?

Be assured that God will honor what He has promised in His Word no matter what the time frame may be, whether you live to see it fulfilled or not.

Are there substantial promises in Scripture which extend to our children? The answer is, "Yes!"

On the Day of Pentecost Peter promised that the gift of the Holy Spirit was "for you and your children and for all who are far off—for all whom the Lord our God will call" (Acts 2:39). When the jailer at Philippi was concerned about his own safety (jailers who had prisoners escape during their watch could lose their lives as punishment), Paul and Silas said, "Believe in the Lord Jesus, and you will be saved—you and your household" (Acts 16:31). The Roman household included not only children but servants as well.

God will honor what He has promised in His Word whether you live to see it fulfilled or not.

These promises, of course, don't deny the child the freedom of choice, or eliminate the stubborn will of a youngster who wants a taste of the world. Nor does it suggest that your children do not have to make the same transactions of faith that you had to make, but it does give you as a parent confidence to trust God in the meanwhile.

If you need further encouragement, let me share one more thought with you. In the Old Testament are two passages that ask the question, "Is there anything too hard for the Lord?" Those two passages are Genesis 18:14 and Jeremiah 32:27. Both of these passages are followed by promises that extend to our children. Is it merely a coincidence? Or is God saying specifically that nothing is too hard for Him, including changing the stubborn will of a prodigal son or daughter, and pointing that one back toward home and heaven?

> ### INSIGHT
>
> *When you pray for your children to follow the Lord, you can be sure that you are praying for God's will (see 1 Timothy 2:4; 2 Peter 3:9; Acts 2:39 and Acts 16:31), so you can pray in faith, trusting Him.*

When Judah and his brothers went to Egypt and the youngest, Benjamin, was detained, Judah, who took responsibility for the lad, asked, "How shall I go up to my father, and the lad be not with me?" (Genesis 44:34, *KJV*). That's a question every parent must ask in relationship to our heavenly Father, "How shall I go up to my Father, at the end of life, and my children not be with me?" Think about it.

THINK ON THIS

1   If you believe God will honor His Word
    regarding your family, don't say, "My son is
    not a Christian." Rather in faith say, "My
    son hasn't yet trusted the Lord but I am
    confident that he will."

2   If you came to Christ after your children
    were grown, after much prayer sit down
    with them. Let them know that you didn't
    know the Lord when they were growing
    up, which accounted for your failure to
    introduce them to spiritual things. Explain
    that now that you have become a Christian,
    you would very much like them to discover
    the same thing for themselves.

RESOURCE READING

Joshua 24:14-27

A FINAL WORD

The TV show *Who Wants to Be a Millionaire?* made famous the question, "Is that your final answer?" For us who are parents, only God has the final answer. The good news is that He does have the answer, and when we get to the end of our capabilities and there still seems to be no answers, we can quietly say, "God, we need Your help! We aren't sure what to do!"

A famous father in the Old Testament whose son attempted to wrest the kingdom from him cried out, "When my heart is overwhelmed: lead me to the rock that is higher than I" (Psalm 61:2, *KJV*). God met David's need, and He will meet yours as well.

Raising kids is much like crossing a river. When you are out there in the current, you wonder if you are ever going to get across.

But you will! And God will be with you each step of the way!

Yes, we have no alternative but to confront our culture if we are going to protect our kids from what can sweep them downstream to Sodom. Someday you will look back and reminisce. You will not trade the tears, the joys and the experiences of watching your child grow into maturity for anything in the world. It is one of the truly great experiences of life. May God make those years as precious and meaningful to you as they have been for my wife, Darlene and me. Keep your Bible and the band-aids handy! They are both necessary. And enjoy the journey of parenting.

ENDNOTES

1   Glenn Doman, personal correspondence with the author, September 20, 2000.

2   "How Could This Happen?" *The Denver Post*, April 25, 1999, Section H, p. 1.

3   John Drescher, *If I Were Starting My Family Again* (Intercourse, PA: Good Books, 1994), n.p.

4   Laura Schlessinger as quoted by Ross Werland, "Should You Spy on Your Teen?" *Reader's Digest*, July 2000, p. 160.

5   Kathi Kemper, MD, "ADHD, or Another Problem?" Available: http://onhealth.com/ch1/columnist/item,35494.asp, March 15, 2000.

6   Joan Hansen, "Chess Champ Takes on Newhart's Best," *Saddleback Valley News*, March 15, 2000, p. 3.

7   Kathi Kemper, MD, "ADHD Changes Begin at Home," Available: http://onhealth.com/ch1/columnist/item,35504.asp, January 2, 1999.

8   Theresa Walker, "Parents vs. Peers," *The Orange County Register*, September 15, 1998, Accent, p. 1.

9   Used by permission of Family First, Inc., Tampa, FL.

10 Carolyn Poirot, "Sudden Mood Swings Called Clues to Abuse," *Fort Worth Star-Telegram*, October 28, 1984 as quoted by Zig Ziglar in *Raising Positive Kids in a Negative World* (New York: Balantine Books, 1996), p. 184.

11 Ziglar, p. 191.

12 From the author's book *Tomorrow Starts Today*, October 14 selection, used by permission of Barbour Publishers, Uhrichville, Ohio, 1999.

13 *Ibid.*, February 24 selection, used by permission of Barbour Publishers, Uhrichville, Ohio, 1999.

14 *Ibid.*, February 25 selection, used by permission of Barbour Publishers, Uhrichville, Ohio, 1999.

15 Ron Stodghill II, "Where'd You Learn That?" *Time*, June 15, 1998, Vol. 151, No. 23., pp. 52-60.

16 *Ibid.*

17 Available: http://hlthed.sask.com/cni/unit/10.4.2/tbsui_103.html, November 16, 2000.

18 Sharrel Keyes, "To Choose to Live—Why Suicide is Not for Me," *His*, January 1980, p. 7.

If we can provide further help, contact us. You can write or send e-mail to the following:

In Asia:

Dr. Harold J. Sala
Guidelines International Ministries
Box 4000
Makati, Metro Manila
Philippines

In the United States:

Dr. Harold J. Sala
Guidelines International Ministries
Box G
Laguna Hills, CA 92654
www.guidelines.org
E-mail: guidelines@guidelines.org

While God can use this book
to draw you to know the truth,
you can discover for yourself the ultimate
source of Truth—God's Word, The Bible.
Read it today!

*"All Scripture is inspired by God and is useful to teach us
what is true and to make us realize what is wrong
in our lives. It straightens us out and teaches us
to do what is right."* 2 Timothy 3:16 NLT

We would love
to hear from you!

**Please share with us how this book
has helped or blessed you.**

For your comments and suggestions:

Email us at info@omflit.com

or

Call us at 531-6635

or

Text **OMFLIT**<space><TITLE OF BOOK>
<your comments> and send to 2299

OMF LITERATURE INC.
Publishing Truth.
Shaping Generations.
www.OMFLit.com